CHRISTINE WOOD

THE BURDENS WE CARRY

HOW TO LIVE FREELY AND LIGHTLY
IN A WEARY AND BURDENED WORLD

© 2025 by Christine Wood

livingwithmargins.com

All rights reserved. No part of this book may be reproduced in any form, stored in a retrieval system, or transmitted in any form by any means—electronic, mechanical, photocopy, recording or otherwise—without the prior written permission of the author, except as provided by Australian copyright law.

Unless otherwise noted, all scripture quotations are taken from the Holy Bible, New International Version®, NIV® Copyright © 1973, 1978, 1984, 2011 by Biblica, Inc.® Used by permission. All rights reserved worldwide.

This book was written solely by the author without the assistance of artificial intelligence (AI) tools or software.

Edited by Chelsea Slade – chelseaslade.com

Cover design and typeset by Jordan Bariesheff – jordanbariesheff.com

ISBN 978-1-7640688-0-2

*For my girls: Kate, Amy, and Leah.
May you never struggle under the weight of burdens
you were never meant to carry.*

And for Murray. My darling, this is our story.

Come to me, all you who are weary and burdened, and I will give you rest.

—Jesus,
Matthew 11:28

CONTENTS

Introduction   9
   I'm Fine, Everything's Fine
   Until It's Not

1 Everybody's Doing It   17
   The Burdened Life Is Normal

2 Things Have To Change   29
   The Burden Of Feeling Stuck

3 Welcome To The Rat Race   45
   The Burden Of Busyness

4 Girls Can Do Anything   61
   The Burden Of Unrealistic
   Expectations

5 Penny For Your Thoughts   75
   The Burden Of Worry

6 Am I Not Pretty Enough?   89
   The Burden Of Physical Appearance

7 Mistakes, Regrets &
**   Embarrassing Moments**   105
   The Burden Of Striving For God's Love

8 Bigger Is Better   119
   The Burden Of Our Possessions

9 Do More, Be Better   133
   The Burden Of Limited Capacity

10 Good Girl Christian 151
   The Burden Of Religion

11 Everyone Is Hurting 165
   The Burden Of Suffering

12 A New Beginning 181
   Learning To Live Freely And Lightly

Notes 194

About The Author 199

INTRODUCTION

I'M FINE, EVERYTHING'S FINE

UNTIL IT'S NOT

It was Friday morning in the church office. We were all rushing around with final preparations for the conference beginning that evening. I was the Discipleship Pastor at the time, and I had my team of life group leaders coming to a training workshop the following day. Everything was on track. I was just finishing off the slide show for my team training. Vision Conference was always a highlight on the calendar, setting the vision for the busy year of ministry ahead.

It began as a dull ache, barely distinguishable. A pressure

in my chest. By late morning the pressure had increased to an uncomfortable pain, gradually growing worse. My fingers began to tingle, and I felt like I had a pile of bricks pushing on my chest.

So I ate some lunch and went back to work on my slide show.

But ignoring the pain didn't make it go away. This was very inconvenient. It was just hours before the conference was due to begin. My team was counting on me. I had a key role in the pastoral team of our large church. I was doing a great job. Our teams and leaders were growing; ministry was going well. I was innovating, improving, and making key changes to take our discipleship program to the next level. This was not a good day to have a heart attack.

But as I sat at my desk, trying to ignore the pain in my chest, the tingles in my arms and hands, and the lightheaded feeling, I thought of my family. How would I explain to my husband I had ignored the pain in my chest for five hours before calling for help? My kids deserved better. It wasn't about me anymore. Both of my parents had experienced heart issues. Was it my turn? It was foolish to continue to ignore the pain.

Eventually, I asked a trusted colleague to call an ambulance for me.

I was embarrassed, suddenly the centre of attention. The paramedics took my vital signs and gave me medication for the pain. They asked me what seemed like a hundred questions. Soon they strapped me to a trolley and wheeled me into the ambulance.

The doctors in emergency were professional and kind. I was given more strong painkillers and attached to a heart monitor. Later that evening, I was admitted into coronary care for monitoring and tests. The pain didn't go away.

The next four days were some of the hardest of my life. There were rounds of uncomfortable and invasive tests. I was woken early every morning by nurses taking blood. I hated being in hospital. I felt powerless and vulnerable. At any time, day or night, random strangers would come into my room for some test or another, accessing the well-positioned openings on my gown to put stickers and chords on my chest. I was exposed and completely disarmed. I had X-rays, ECGs, an ultrasound, and a CAT scan. And still, the pain didn't go away. Eventually, my heart was given a clean bill of health. In fact, my heart is in excellent health with no signs of the problems either of my parents had.

I was sent home with a diagnosis of panic attack.

There was nothing wrong with me. It was all just stress. This was the last thing I wanted. You see, I knew I was under a lot of pressure. I knew there was a lot going on. But I thought I was handling it. If you had asked me how I was going, I would have told you I was coping okay. I was fine.

But my body wasn't fine. I wasn't fine at all.

I was put on a mental health plan and sent to see a counsellor. She advised me to have a month off work. I was back in the office a week later. Looking back, I don't know why I didn't have the time off she suggested. I guess I didn't believe how sick I was. I thought I could just keep going but be less stressed. I was so wrong.

Jesus said, "Come to me, all you who are weary and burdened, and I will give you rest".[1] Jesus promised abundant life. Jesus promised peace. And while I appeared to live a peaceful, abundant life on the surface, deep underneath, I was struggling. I was weary and burdened. It wasn't until I began to buckle under the weight that Jesus began to show me I was carrying burdens He never intended me to hold.

This incident was a symptom of a mindset I carried with

me all my life. My life was perfect on the outside. But on the inside, I was a mess. I never felt like I was good enough. I struggled with worry and anxiety. I was tired but just kept pushing. I was always afraid of letting someone down. I tried to do everything right, and I tried to keep everyone happy. And it nearly killed me.

When I sat with Jesus in the days after my hospital visit, the dull ache much improved but still heavy in my chest, Jesus spoke words of comfort and peace to my soul. He reminded me He loves me because of who I am, not because of what I can do for Him. He gave me permission to rest.

It took me another nine months, but eventually, I did rest. I walked away from over ten years in ministry, all my friends, and my comfortable, programmed church life. Then, I began to lay down the burdens, one by one.

I discovered the burdens of my heart came from three sources:

1. **My own expectations.** I believed I should behave a certain way, do certain things, and be a certain way.
2. **The church's expectations.** The church, both implicitly and explicitly, preaches to us about what a good Christian woman should be like. And it is very convincing! We have a list of shoulds to keep up with and role models to aspire to.
3. **The world I live in.** The culture we live in preaches its own list of expectations. Women should look a certain way; we should work and study and start our own businesses. We should be smashing glass ceilings and taking our place in the world.

The weight of these expectations is heavy.

***

Because I had my chest pain and hospital visit on the day of our church conference, there was no hiding it or keeping it private. It became very public very quickly. While I was in hospital, the church prayed for me, publicly from stage. And when I returned, everyone I spoke to in the church foyer wanted to know the whole story.

I would have preferred to say, "I had a heart attack" than "I had a panic attack." I have pastorally walked with many people who struggled with their mental health. I didn't think I held a stigma against mental health challenges. But here I was, embarrassed about my own diagnosis.

What I didn't expect was the avalanche of comments from people who said, "That happened to me too." It turns out that stress-induced chest pain is common, and a lot of people at some stage in their lives have a similar experience. There is an epidemic of stress in our world. And there is an epidemic of stress in our churches. I'm not alone in struggling under the weight of striving to live the right way and do all the right things.

What are we getting so wrong? If Jesus said, "My yoke is easy and my burden is light", why are we stressed out to the point of collapse? My only conclusion: my expectations are different to Jesus' expectations. What I am carrying is not the yoke of discipleship Jesus designed for me.

As I explored Scripture, sitting at Jesus' feet, crying out in frustration and pain, completely broken, I began to recognise the burdens I was carrying that were not a part of Jesus' plan for me. And as I learned to put them down, I discovered a peace and joy that felt like the *'rest for your soul'* Jesus promised.

In the days after my panic attack diagnosis, I spent a lot of time praying and journalling. I practised the meditation and mindfulness exercises my doctor recommended. I listened to podcasts and read books. I cried a lot. And while nothing obvious changed in the first few months, there was a shift deep inside me. I knew something was fundamentally wrong with my life and I knew something needed to change, even though I didn't know what or how.

As I worked with my counsellor over the following weeks, and as I sat with God and put it all on the table, I began to reassess my life. It was the beginning of the most beautiful journey of my life.

***

If you picked up this book, I'm guessing you would put yourself in the *'weary and burdened'* category too. You feel like the weight of the world is on your shoulders, and it's starting to get heavy. Or perhaps, like me, you've begun to crumble, and you know you need to change how you're living, but you're not sure what to do or how to do it.

This book is going to walk you through, step by step, how to lay down your burdens. We will look one by one at the expectations we put on ourselves that weigh us down. We will explore the truth of what Scripture teaches us about each of these expectations, and look at simple, practical strategies to learn a new way of thinking and a new way of living.

We will explore the expectations of our Christian culture, and how there are attitudes that have evolved over time and mixed with our modern culture that present us with a to-do-list faith rather than a relational faith. I love Jesus, and I love the Church. This book is not anti-church. But we will explore how some theology has been twisted out of balance to make us think and do things differently from how Jesus intended.

And we will cast a critical eye over how culture lies to us about what is important and valuable in life. We are bombarded with messages and images of what a happy, successful woman is like. This story is told in such an attractive and convincing way, we begin to believe it and internalise it without even recognising that the message is a lie.

Over the course of this book, we will explore the burdens we carry—burdens I am learning to put down. You may recognise all of them, or perhaps just a few. We are all different. But I hope and pray you will notice your own burdens and name them for what they truly are: not part of God's design for your life. And I pray you will learn to lay them down, so you too can discover what living freely and lightly really feels like.

In John 10:10, Jesus said, "I have come that they may have life, and have it to the full" (NIV). The NLT describes it as 'a rich and satisfying life'. The KJV translates it as 'abundant life'. This is the kind of life Jesus promised! Full, rich, satisfying, and abundant. This is real life in relationship with God.

Let's not settle for a *weary and burdened* life. Let's not ignore the warning signs and continue to struggle on, dissatisfied and overwhelmed, stressed and tired. Let's accept Jesus' promise of rest for our souls and live life to the full. Together, we can.

1

EVERYBODY'S DOING IT

THE BURDENED LIFE IS NORMAL

Bzzzz, bzzzz, bzzzz. My phone starts vibrating softly on my bedside table. Soon it will begin to chime, growing louder until I turn it off. It's time for another day to begin.

I push the double shot button on the coffee machine and grab my Bible. Flicking to the next part of the chapter where I left off yesterday, I read a few familiar verses, take a deep breath and exhale a prayer, "Lord, guide my day."

I jump in the shower then blow-dry my hair, especially

the front bit that sticks up like a fountain on my forehead if I don't style it carefully. Makeup on, I stand in front of my open wardrobe and try to decide what to wear. What is on my to-do list today? What do I feel like wearing? Eventually I grab my most comfortable black pants and a shirt, only to change the shirt twice more, carefully adjusting my front tuck, before slipping on my shoes, grabbing the car keys and a supermarket meal out of the freezer and heading into morning peak-hour traffic.

Forty minutes later I duck into the back of the staff prayer meeting. I'm a little late, but I know I won't be the last to arrive. I take a deep breath and exhale my prayer, "Lord, guide my day."

I love my office. When I stepped into this new role as Discipleship Pastor, having my own office and a small stipend to decorate it was a wonderful blessing. The walls are pale grey, there are white bookshelves laden with the wisdom of my favourite authors, a large print on the wall next to the printed calendar of the church year, colour-coded with events and deadlines. I sit down, close the office door and examine my to-do list. "Lord, guide my day."

In between meetings, I tick tasks off the list. I make calls, send emails, and answer questions. But no matter how many tasks I complete or projects I move forward, I seem to have just as many, or often even more, still on the list at the end of the day.

Sitting in traffic on the way home, I have the radio turned up, listening to silly banter and mind-numbing music. I wish I could have gotten more done today. I never seem to have enough time. And just when one deadline is met, a new one is looming. If only I could just get a little bit ahead. Maybe then I would be able to follow my boss's advice and "Work smarter, not harder."

I'm exhausted.

I cook a simple dinner, we watch the next episode of whatever series we are watching on Netflix and fall into bed.

And do it again tomorrow.

I hope the story of my day didn't bore you too much. Because, if you're anything like most of my friends, I probably described your day too, give or take a few details. I know there are variations. Getting children up and ready for school, with lunches and hats and homework in tow. We have groceries to buy and doctors' appointments to make and elderly parents to visit. You may fit in a session at the gym or an evening class. But chances are, you end your day exhausted with more on your to-do list than you had the day before. It's endless, and the proverbial light at the end of the tunnel is too far away to see from here.

This is the normal way to live. This is how everyone lives. What choice do we have?

I'm sitting in my favourite coffee shop as I write, in a row of other people with a laptop on the table and a coffee at their elbow. It's a lovely environment to work in when I want a change from working at home alone. Here we have a shared experience, even though we never speak. Looking around I wonder, did they have to carefully style the front section of their hair too? How many shirts did they try on before they ran out the door this morning? How do they feel about their growing to-do list and relentless pace? Do they also finish their day with the sinking feeling of not having accomplished quite enough, again?

In December 2022, an Australian Community Survey undertaken by NCLS Research found that 64% of Australians rated their stress as 5 out of 10 or above, while 40% rated their stress levels at 7 or above.[2]

In a 2024 survey of 534 Baptist women in leadership

across Australia, of which I am one, 42% said they were satisfied with their ministry but found it draining, 38% reported having high levels of stress, and 62% admitted they considered quitting ministry.[3]

That's an awful lot of women feeling stressed. That's an awful lot of church leaders at the end of their rope, carefully considering their future in ministry.

Feeling drained and stressed is more and more normal. And it's not just in Australia, and not just among church leaders. It's everywhere.

We prioritise productivity over health and happiness. We prioritise our to-do list over our relationships. We read books about stress management and call it self-care. We spend our lives striving to lose weight and pay bills. Sigh. And then we layer on the expectations of our faith because we are not just trying to get it all done; we are trying to do it all the right way, honouring God and serving our community selflessly.

It's a lot to juggle. And many of us have been living like this for a very long time.

***

It was the early nineties—an age ago, I know, but in many ways, it feels like yesterday. I was twenty-five, newly married and about to have children. The books I was reading then were teaching me how to do everything right and keep everyone happy. I'd grown up a pastor's kid, the eldest of four daughters. I was labelled 'bossy' because I was a typical eldest child. I was also insecure and always struggled to feel like I fit in.

When our children were small, I secretly felt like a failure as a mother and a homemaker. Our home was often messy and unorganised. I struggled to keep up with the laundry.

We seemed to spend hours each day looking for things we'd lost. I read books about parenting and home organisation. We didn't have a lot of money in those early years. I blamed my discontent on the small rental homes we lived in and dreamed of having a big, beautiful home one day.

But the big, beautiful home didn't solve the problem. So I read books about home decoration and styling and invested in home organisation systems. They didn't help much either.

I was stuck. It was like driving at top speed on a multi-lane highway. I was part of the crowd, living my life the best I knew how, following the road to success as fast as I could. My life was perfect on the outside. I was married to a loving, godly man. I had three healthy children and a cute little dog. We were part of a great church. We had supportive friends and family around us. Why did I feel so miserable? I had no right to be unhappy.

It wasn't until my perfect life started unravelling, and we were forced to take an exit ramp off that freeway to success, that we discovered there was a different way to live. I wasn't really a failure. I was just failing at living up to an arbitrary set of expectations God never intended for me to follow in the first place.

That's how I got to a Friday in February, sitting at my desk with the pain heavy on my chest, pain I ignored for five hours because I was desperately trying to get everything done. Despite having a family history of heart disease. Despite having a family to go home to. I pushed the obvious needs of my body aside to keep up the game—do everything right, keep everyone happy.

It was the day of Vision Conference. It was the kick-start event of the year. It was a big deal, an important day. And I had an important role. Our network of Life Groups was led by dedicated volunteers who were also busy and stressed. They had committed to attending this training day to improve their knowledge and skills to be the best group leaders they could be, and they were relying on me to help them do that. This was not a good day to have a heart attack. So I ignored the pain. Until I couldn't.

It was only later, after four days in hospital, that I discovered the real source of my pain: my body wasn't coping with the stress I was carrying. I had a panic attack.

As I write this, remembering the experience, I can feel my chest tighten. I can feel my breath quicken. I still have a physical reaction to the memory. My body is not detached from the stress. My body and mind are not just connected; they are one.

I didn't know stress could cause intense physical pain like that. I thought mental illness was for people who couldn't cope. I was so wrong. I thought I was coping well, but I was emotionally and mentally exhausted. I thought I was handling everything, but my body told another story.

On Monday evening, my husband, Murray, picked me up from the coronary care unit and brought me home. I was so tired. Four days in hospital were not restful at all.

I felt a mixture of emotions. I was relieved I didn't have heart problems. I saw what my father went through when he had heart surgery and, although the surgery was successful and he recovered well, I didn't want to go through that myself. But I didn't want the diagnosis of anxiety or panic attack either. It felt harder. The solution was less clear. With a heart attack, you go on medication, adopt a low-fat, low-salt diet, and exercise more. With a panic attack, I wasn't sure what to do. I went to my GP, who gave me a certificate for time off work, and I made an appointment to see a counsellor.

Those were hard days. The chest pain proved that I wasn't coping with my life. But I didn't know how to fix it. By the end of the week, I didn't want to stay at home anymore. Even though my family and work colleagues encouraged me to take more time to rest, and even though I had accrued weeks of sick leave, I felt an expectation. An expectation to keep pushing as hard as I could. An expectation to get over it and get on with it. An expectation not to let things slip any further; to keep all the balls I was juggling in the air. Because the longer I was away from work, the more emails would be in my inbox on my return. The closer the project deadlines would loom, the longer the to-do list, the more people I would disappoint.

And, just to be clear, every one of these expectations was my own. Not one person—my boss, my team, my colleagues or church—said one word that gave me the impression I was letting them down if I took more time off to recover. No. All the expectations to keep pushing were my own. I wanted to prove I was capable.

I could still feel the dull ache in my chest, but now I knew what it was: it was just stress. So, determined to manage it better, I went back to work.

Many people don't take the time off they are entitled to. A 2023 survey of U.S. workers found that 46% of employees did not take the vacation time their employer allowed. Two of the most common reasons given were that they were worried they would fall behind and that they felt bad about their co-workers needing to take on additional responsibilities to cover for them.

A 2022 Harvard Business Review article summarising Gallup's latest State of the Global Workplace report is alarmingly titled, "Stressed, Sad, and Anxious: A Snapshot of the Global Workforce."[4]

Jump forward a couple of years and the situation hasn't improved. The 2024 report opens with this quote from the

United Nations Development Programme:

> *And further still, people's mental wellbeing has been worsening. In the last 10 years, the number of people expressing stress, sadness, anxiety, anger or worry has been on the rise, reaching its highest levels since the Gallup surveys began.*[5]

That's since 1935. That's a long time ago. We are stressed, sad, anxious, angry, and worried.

I can relate. This is how I felt.

As a Christian, I was deeply uncomfortable with the disconnect between what Jesus said His followers' lives should be like and my lived experience. Where is the peace Jesus promised, the peace that passes understanding? Jesus promised us abundant life, and we are stressed, sad, and anxious. Jesus invites us to come to Him to find rest for our soul, and yet we are still on the 'weary and burdened' side of the equation. Is Jesus' promise just for Heaven? Is it possible to experience an abundant life here and now?

One thing is for sure; in order to experience the abundant life, peace that passes understanding and rest for our souls, we can't continue to live a normal life. We have to make changes. We have to live differently.

The world's solution is the explosion of the wellness industry. There are popular apps such as Headspace and Calm. Yoga studios are popping up in every suburb. There is a place across the street from my apartment building where you can do float therapy in an Epsom salt pool in a dark, quiet room, promising "a deep state of relaxation, so your brain can enter a place of rest and repair."[6] Sounds lovely. I tried it once and didn't really enjoy it, but I know many people who swear by it. These solutions can be beneficial for our mental health, but they haven't solved the problem of the mental health crisis. They don't provide the deep soul rest we so desperately long for.

But Jesus can.

Hindsight is a beautiful gift. I can look back now at the most difficult seasons of my life and clearly see how God was guiding me away from my misguided value system and gently drawing me to Himself. The panic attack I experienced was the wake-up call I needed. It forced me to search Scripture, spend more time in prayer and seek professional help. And it shone a spotlight on past life lessons I needed to re-learn and incorporate into my life.

There is a line in Joni Mitchell's well-known song, *Big Yellow Taxi*, that talks about not knowing what you have until it's gone. I proved that to be true, but not in a negative sense. Rather, I didn't know how heavy the burdens I was carrying through life were until I began to put them down.

When I stopped dressing up for work, blow-drying my hair and covering my face with makeup every day, I discovered the toxic relationship I had with my body.

When I stopped going to church for three services every Sunday, I discovered a religious spirit, striving to impress people rather than connect with God.

When I slowed down, taking time for unhurried conversations and long walks in nature and allowing myself time to be bored, I discovered connection, creativity and joy.

Away from my to-do list, away from my roles as mother and pastor, removed from a lifetime of expectations and insecurities, I discovered a new way to live, and it challenged everything I thought was normal in the past.

I discovered the reality of the abundant life Jesus talked about. His yoke truly is easy; His burden is truly light—just like He said.

We can accept Jesus' invitation to bring our weary and burdened hearts to Him and find rest for our souls. When we take on His yoke, and only His yoke, we find that it is so much lighter than the weight of the world's expectations we carry. Abundant life is something we can enjoy when we reject the false value system of the world, redefine success in line with God's Word, and surrender our expectations to our Saviour.

We can live slowly in a world going at breakneck speed.

We can find our unique purpose and follow our dreams in a world that expects us to do everything.

We can trust God confidently with the concerns of our hearts and exchange our worried thoughts for peace.

We can love our bodies in a world that worships youth and beauty.

We can live within our limited capacity, at peace with the fact we will never do enough to keep everybody happy.

We can overcome our feelings of guilt and shame, living in the freedom of unconditional love and forgiven sin.

We can live simply in a world that values excess.

We can be devoted followers of Jesus and contribute to His church without sacrificing our mental health and well-being.

We can care for the hurting without drowning in their pain.

And we can take control and change our lives. We can exit the world's freeway to fake success and find the path Jesus has marked out for us.

We can live freely and lightly in a weary and burdened world.

Let's get started.

2

THINGS HAVE TO CHANGE

THE BURDEN OF FEELING STUCK

We were on vacation visiting my parents in Central Queensland, sitting in a local coffee shop, sharing a vanilla slice. It was the Easter holidays of 2019, about a year before the panic attack.

"How would you feel about taking a year off and driving around Australia in a caravan?" Murray asked.

It was completely out of the blue. He had never shown any interest in caravanning. We'd never been much into camping or long road trips. We both had busy full-time jobs, friends, commitments and obligations, not to mention three kids in their twenties who were only just establishing themselves independently.

At the time I made an offhand, "That sounds nice" reply, thinking it wasn't real. It was just one of those crazy dreams you have on vacation that evaporates when you return to real life. Except this dream didn't evaporate; it grew clearer and stronger. A couple of months after returning home, we found ourselves at the Camping and Caravanning Super Show, walking in and out of hundreds of mobile homes of all different shapes and sizes, getting a feel for what life on the road might be like.

And we started talking to people. We knew a few friends who had done similar things, and as we started conversations, we found plenty of people who were happy to talk to us about their experiences. The thing most of these people had in common was a story of tragedy that prompted them to re-evaluate their lives and do something they had always wanted before it was too late. The message was loud and clear: life is short; don't waste it doing something other than what you love.

Not one person we talked to regretted their decision to travel. Every single one said it was the best thing they had ever done. And this crazy idea picked up momentum.

I cannot emphasise enough how truly out of character this idea was for us. We were very, very normal. We were not adventurous people. Murray was driving a Mercedes coupe sports car. When we went away for weekends, we enjoyed the theatre, shopping malls and fine dining. We were living in the middle of the city, and we were very comfortable with our very urban life. Doing a lap, as we call it here Down Under, was a world away from anything we had ever known.

But we couldn't shake the excitement and hope that filled

us with every conversation we had, every YouTube we watched and every camping store we visited. We were hungry to change our lives. We were hungry to do something different.

The hardest part of contemplating this trip, for me, was our children. They were 22, 24 and 25 at the time. And my mother's heart couldn't reconcile the idea of leaving them. Our two girls had already flown the nest, and their lives were swimming along fine, but our youngest, our son, was still living with us. Is it okay to kick out your youngest child to go away on an adventure? I cried every time I even thought about it. But they all wanted this for us as much as we needed it for ourselves. They were ready to grow up. They had each other (and loads of friends and extended family) and were happy to see us go.

The lease on our rental apartment was due to finish in October 2020. So, with plenty of time up our sleeves, we began to make plans to have a one-year break from the busyness and stress of life to travel.

When I had my panic attack, I knew I had to make some changes, but I didn't want to be rash and reactionary. I didn't want to admit defeat and give in to the urge to just quit. I planned to continue on, but with an improved productivity system to help me manage everything better. And, I had October to look forward to when our caravan adventure would begin.

Then, in March 2020, the whole world changed. Everything was turned upside down. All sense of normality disappeared. We all learned to work from home and pastor a church remotely. I held the virtual hands of our church's Life Group leaders as we learned how to do pastoral care and discipleship through a screen and over the phone. All of a sudden, stress, worry, fear and anxiety were the norm for every single person I knew, and we all went into survival mode together.

By the time October arrived, rather than taking leave, Murray and I both resigned from our jobs. We weren't sure how long we were going to be away, but we realised we didn't want a deadline.

Eighteen months after the crazy conversation in the coffee shop that I fobbed off as a dream, we were on the road. We sold and gave away almost everything. We kept a few boxes of our most precious possessions and a couple of pieces of furniture we loved in storage, and a twenty-one-foot caravan became our home.

And the son we abandoned, (we didn't really abandon him, but it did feel like it at the time,) thrived.

Thrived.

The next two and a half years became the adventure of our lifetime. We travelled the width and breadth of our beautiful country. We discovered who we were outside of the roles of parents and employees. We discovered what faith looked like outside of the programs of an organised church. We discovered each other again, thirty years after we were married. We learned what life could be like with the most simple and basic material possessions. And we discovered what relationships could be like when time constraints and work pressures didn't exist.

It was the perfect circuit-breaker for us. Murray and I were both exhausted by the weight of our lives. We knew something had to change, and rather than making tiny incremental changes, trying to continue to survive in the middle of the rapids, we got out of the water. It was hard at first. It's hard to stop when you are used to the relentless hustle. But after a while, we discovered a new pace of life, a new joy, and a new peace that ran deep.

I started to laugh again—spontaneous, joy-overflowing laughter. I slept longer and more soundly. I became braver, willing to try new things and have a go at experiences I would have previously been comfortable just watching. I hiked into national parks, swam under waterfalls, walked on remote beaches and learned to knit socks.

And I had space for new ideas. I wrote my first devotional book and three guided journals while we were on the road, answers to prayers that lay stagnant in my heart for years. When the pressure and busyness of day-to-day life and ministry were taken away, I could finally do the things I had been dreaming of.

This was a monumental change. We turned our entire lives upside down. It is the best thing we ever did, and I don't regret a day of it. But this wasn't the answer to all our problems. And it isn't the answer to your overburdened life. We can't all sell all our possessions, move into an RV and travel full-time. It's not practical. I don't expect you to follow my example unless it is something you definitely want to do.

Most people I know who struggle under the pace of a relentless life take a few weeks of stress leave and then return to work and continue much the same as before. I've seen it so many times among friends and colleagues. They come back to work feeling refreshed and determined, and a month or two later the clouds begin to threaten once again. They dream of their next vacation. They are back in survival mode.

***

When I was young, we used to play a game called 'Stuck in the Mud'. It was a variation of tiggy. When we were tagged, we couldn't move until someone who was free scrambled under our legs. Then we could run again. I was never a good runner, so I usually spent most of the game standing still, legs wide apart, yelling at my friends to come and set me free. Without them, I was stuck.

There is nothing worse than the feeling of being stuck, with no options and no way out. Some seasons and circumstances make us feel trapped. But I am here to testify that God will always provide a way for us to escape or persevere.

I had my three kids close together. There are three years and five months between the oldest and the youngest, with one more in between. The early years were unrelenting. I was a stay-at-home mum, taking care of our children and home full-time. We were a one-car family, so I was quite literally stuck at home all day every day with my babies, apart from one day a week when we bundled the kids into the car early in the morning to drop Murray off at the train station so we could go to playgroup, run errands and do the grocery shopping.

Life felt like an endless treadmill. Days and weeks were the same, filled with mundane tasks: cooking and cleaning, doing unending loads of laundry and entertaining cranky babies and inquisitive toddlers. I am not complaining; I loved those years. I was blessed to become a mother to three healthy children and was blessed to have the freedom to be their primary carer until they went to school. It is what I signed up for. But it was still hard.

The days were long. I've never known exhaustion more than in those early years of parenting. But, as hard as it was, it didn't last forever. My children grew up. They became more and more independent. Eventually, we purchased a second car, and I could enjoy the free hours while they were in school so I could run errands and pursue other interests. It was a season. And seasons pass. Before I knew it, there were three cars on the street outside my home with young adults coming and going to their jobs and universities, only coming home for free food and clean clothes. The season changed.

God gave me the strength I needed to persevere through the hectic years of parenting our three children. But sometimes, the circumstances we find ourselves stuck in don't change by themselves. Sometimes, we don't need perseverance. Sometimes, we need the courage to change our lives.

A few months ago, I was invited back to our old church for the special retirement service for our pastor. It was so lovely to catch up with friends I hadn't seen in years. I had conversations that delighted and inspired me as I saw young people who had grown up, now in leadership and ministry positions in the church. There were weddings and babies and graduations to celebrate. And then, other conversations left me discouraged. Some friends were complaining about the same things in the same circumstances they were working through fifteen years earlier. They hadn't moved forward. Nothing had changed.

I know someone who, every time I speak to her, complains about the length of her commute. And yet, more than ten years later, she lives in the same place. I have a colleague who, after returning from being on the mission field for many years, is finding it difficult to make friends. And yet, she always has excuses as to why she can't join a church connect group or community club. Nothing suits her. So she keeps complaining about not having any friends.

It's so sad, but it happens all the time. We get caught on the treadmill of life with a job we hate, a family conflict to manage or a home that doesn't suit us, and we are paralysed to change. We can't see how. We're stuck in the mud. But it doesn't have to be this way.

We have a God who is in the business of making a way where there is no way. Scripture is littered with examples. I think of Daniel in the lions' den; David facing Goliath; Joshua marching his troops around Jericho; Shadrach,

Meshach and Abednego standing in the furnace; and Elisha asking the widow to share her last meal. In every case, there was no way forward. But in all of these instances, God does a supernatural miracle and makes a way where there is no way.

But there is one story of escape that tops the list. Do you remember the story of Exodus when Moses led the Children of Israel out of slavery in Egypt? Moses is my Bible hero. God uses him to show His strength, decimating Egypt with plagues to miraculously save His people. To draw a line under the rescue, God makes a way for the people to walk through the Red Sea on dry land, a wall of water on either side. Can you imagine walking that path? Four hundred years of slavery behind, the Promised Land ahead. You might expect the Israelites to be full of faith in their powerful God and excited about the hope of the Promised Land ahead of them. But it didn't pan out that way.

A few months later, following a pillar of cloud by day and a pillar of fire by night, the people arrived at the edge of the Promised Land. Twelve community leaders were chosen to go ahead and spy out the land. Two said, "It's amazing. Let's go!" But ten said, "The people there are too strong. We're all going to die. We can't move forward." They saw the size of the opposition they had to face and didn't have the faith to take hold of the future God had prepared for them. And so, they spent the next forty years wandering around in the desert, waiting for a whole generation to die.

Forty years.

Forty years of wandering, waiting. Stuck.

That's an awfully long time. What were you doing forty years ago?

Take a moment for the enormity of this tragedy to sink in. God had sent Moses, He had sent plague after plague to Egypt, He had walked them through the ocean and drowned their enemies. They drank water gushing from a rock and ate manna and quail sent from the sky. They could see God's presence with them in a cloud by day and a fire by night. What more could God have done to convince them that He would make a way? But rather than claiming their inheritance, they died in the desert and their children took possession of the Promised Land instead. All they had to do was trust God, but they couldn't see a way forward.

The fact is, you have to go through the desert to get to the Promised Land. There is no other way. Sometimes, to claim the promise God has for us, we need to walk through a season or situation of wilderness. But, as we see in this example of the Israelites, we have choices to make while we are in the desert. We can stay there, wandering in the wilderness, or we can trust God and walk forward.

Like the early years of parenting, sometimes God answers our prayers by giving us the strength we need to persevere through the season. Sometimes, God calls us to follow Him faithfully through an ocean and a battle before we arrive at our Promised Land. But whatever our desert looks like, we are going to need to trust God to make a way forward. It will stretch our faith and require more courage than we can muster on our own.

When we find ourselves in the desert, there are some things we can do that make it better, and some things that make it harder. One of the things the Israelites did all the time, and I am also particularly good at, is whinging.

I feel sorry for Moses. It seems like the people he was rescuing did nothing but whinge and whine and complain. Every time they were hungry or thirsty, lost or confused, they threw a pity party and made their complaints loud and clear. And I can understand it. If I were in the middle of the desert with no water on hand and a family to care for, I would make my concerns known. But even after God miraculously cared for them time and time again, they never learned. They never faced an obstacle and responded by looking to God in faith to see how He would save them.

Another thing the Children of Israel did over and over is long for the past. Every time the journey got hard, they wanted to go back. They didn't remember the hardships of the past, just the benefits, and they longed for the good old days of slavery in Egypt. This is harder for me to relate to, but in all honesty, I do it all the time. I want to go back to living in a spacious, beautiful house. I want to go back to when my children were young, when life was simpler and social media didn't exist. I want to go back.

But, of course, it wasn't trouble-free back then. There was stress and pressure and heartache then too. The past can be romanticised in our memory, and it becomes an excuse to be discontent in the present.

And there were a number of times the Israelites got themselves into terrible trouble by listening to the wrong voices. They allowed themselves to be influenced by people who had no faith and looked for solutions outside of God's plan. Aaron created a golden calf for them to worship when Moses was on top of the mountain talking to God. They listened to the ten faithless spies who talked them out of going into the land. There were other instances of insurrection and revolt against Moses and against God. They never ended well.

We can also be easily influenced by unhelpful voices. 'Influencer' is a job title now. People make a lot of money persuading us to believe in the product or philosophy they are promoting. But not all the voices are helpful. We need to be discerning when we choose the voices we allow into our lives.

I've decided to unfriend and unfollow people from my life.

Sometimes this decision is easy, and sometimes, it's painful. But when we listen to the wrong voices, the consequences can be devastating.

Complaining, longing for the past and listening to the wrong voices can keep us stuck in the desert for longer than we need to be. But how can we get ourselves unstuck? How can we move forward when it feels like we have no options? There are a few things I find helpful.

One of the biggest barriers we need to overcome is knowing what we are aiming for. Often, we simply don't know where our destination is, so rather than move forward, we stay where we are. We somehow get the impression that it is ungodly or against God's will if we have goals, as if our dreams could not possibly be part of God's plan. But what if God put those dreams in our hearts? What if God wants us to have a life full of purpose, doing exactly what we love? What if God is leading us to our own Promised Land? Over and over in the gospels, this is the picture of Jesus I see. He loved to give people the desires of their hearts. He loved to set people free.

In Mark's gospel, there is the story of a blind man sitting by the road, listening to the commotion caused by Jesus passing by. He asked someone nearby, "What's going on?" When he was told that Jesus was walking past, he began to call out. When Jesus stopped to talk to the blind man, Bartimaeus, He explicitly asked, "What do you want me to do for you?"[7]

"Master, I want to see," the man replied. And Jesus granted his request. He gave sight to the blind. Bartimaeus got what he wanted.

There is power in having a goal to aim for. When we know what we want, we can plan steps to move toward it. If Jesus asked you today, "What do you want me to do for you?" what would your answer be? Like Bartimaeus, is there a passionate prayer burning in your heart?

It can be fun to throw around the question, "If you could do anything in the world, what would you love to do? If you knew you couldn't fail, what would you have a go at?" This is the mindset it took for Murray and me to travel around the country in a caravan. It is the reason why I am spending my days writing a book. And it is the reason why I spend my leisure time knitting and quilting. These things bring me joy, they make me feel alive, and they give me a sense of purpose. I feel God's smile when I wake up every day and live a life I enjoy.

God gave the Children of Israel a picture of where they were headed, but sometimes we don't have a clear destination. Sometimes we have to follow God, one step at a time, toward the place He is calling us.

Wayne Cordeiro encourages us:

> *Don't stop dreaming of what your life can yet be... without the fishtailing, without the excess, but with all the fruitfulness. You may never become all that you dream of, but you'll never achieve anything that you don't dream of.*[8]

Dream big dreams, my friend.

When I was young, I didn't have a clear plan. At one stage I wanted to be a nurse, but then I decided to try teaching. After that, I went to Bible college to go into ministry, and now I don't do any of those things, at least, not in the traditional sense. Now I'm a mentor, writer and volunteer at church. But I have discovered that my vocation doesn't define me, and, in a sense, it doesn't matter what I do. I am finding such purpose in concentrating on who I am, instead.

Even with a clear destination, however, when we are in the

desert, thirsty and tired, it's hard to have the energy to find our way out. We can't do it alone. A community of friends, a mentor and a professional counsellor can help. Sometimes we just need someone to talk our problems over with to give us a new perspective and a clearer way forward.

I've had a friend who was so burned out and stressed they didn't have the capacity to make changes by themselves. They knew they weren't coping; they knew something needed to change, but they couldn't work it out alone. They were beaten down by life, stuck in survival mode. It took all the energy they had just to get through one more day. They could not see a way forward. They needed good friends around them to hold them up and coach them toward a better future. Looking back now, I'm so proud of how far they've come. They have changed jobs and moved house. They have less pressure at work and a more manageable mortgage. And the spring in their step has returned.

There have been a number of times over the years when I have gone to a counsellor to help get a better perspective on problems I've faced. Whether it was a roadblock in my marriage or parenting or a crisis at work, I couldn't see the way forward by myself. I'm going to share a few of those stories and the helpful advice I was given in future chapters. I've never regretted asking for help when I couldn't see the way forward for myself.

Whether it takes a big, courageous move or a simple attitude adjustment, there is always a way forward with God. He will make a way when we can't find a way.

One of my favourite Psalms is Psalm 40:

> I waited patiently for the Lord; he turned to me and heard my cry. He lifted me out of the slimy pit, out of the mud and mire; he set my feet on a rock and gave me a firm place to stand.[9]

Do you notice how it starts? With us waiting and crying out to God. When we are in a desperate situation, let's not try to solve it ourselves. Let's not turn to secular wisdom to get ourselves out of strife. Wait patiently and cry out to God. Then, "He turned to me and heard my cry." What a blessing. Friend, be assured, God hears your cry. Your pain does not go unnoticed. Your cry does not fall on deaf ears.

God doesn't abandon us when we get stuck. He lifts us out of the slimy pit and gives us a firm place to stand. This is a miracle I know to be true because God has done this for me again and again.

TAKE TIME TO REFLECT

- ☼ Do you feel stuck? Do you look at your life and feel like you have no choices, that there are no other options available to you?

- ☼ Listen to yourself. Do you find yourself talking about the same frustrations over and over again?

- ☼ Is this a season that will change naturally in time? Or are there circumstances you need to change?

Here are some practical steps to lay this burden down:

- Pray. Spend some time praying through Psalm 40. Cry out to God and listen to His guidance.

- Curate the voices you are listening to. Think about who you are being influenced by. Unfollow and unfriend unhelpful voices. Create boundaries with family and friends as needed.

- Dream for the future. Answer Jesus' question, "What do you want me to do for you?" Be brave. It may be as crazy as a trip around Australia in a caravan.

- Ask for help. Who can you talk to who can help you move past your desert season and step into your Promised Land? Plan to talk to a trusted friend, pastor or counselling professional.

3

WELCOME TO THE RAT RACE

THE BURDEN OF BUSYNESS

"Busy day?" the shop assistant asked.

Murray and I were in a lovely little chocolate shop in Adelaide on a weekday.

"No, we don't do busy," Murray answered.

The shop assistant looked puzzled. She didn't know how to respond, as if she had never met anyone who wasn't busy before. Eventually, she replied, "That must be nice."

Everyone is busy. Busy is normal. I know what it's like to be busy, too busy. And I'm sure you do too.

The world we live in glorifies busyness. Being busy is a good thing. It leads to productivity, achievement and success. What are all those hours in the day for if not to fill them up with things to do and places to be?

Busyness is big business. Many productivity systems and programs are designed to help us squeeze the most out of every moment of every day. We have gone from paper planners and to-do lists to digital calendars, where we can book meetings in vacant time slots, share task lists and project plans, and not waste a moment. All of these tools are highly valuable in our productive lives to help us juggle the complexities of our roles and responsibilities.

We value productivity so much that we feel guilty when we sit still. If we are not doing anything productive, we are wasting time, and wasting time is, well, a waste. I recently saw a post on social media that read, "When work is an idol, rest will feel like sin."[10] Whoa, that hits hard!

I'm not sure when it started for me. I wasn't a highly driven teenager. I was quite happy to take time to have fun and cram my assignments into the least amount of time and effort possible. I had three children in three and a half years, and the early years were relentless, as all parents of young children find. I thought I was busy then, and some days were busy, but those early years at home with my babies were a blessed gift. Those years were full of days going at a child's pace, walking to the park, cutting sandwiches into little triangles and picking up toys.

It wasn't until I began working in the church that busyness really hit a new level for me. No matter how hard I worked, how productive I was, or how long after five I stayed at my desk, I never got to the end of my to-do list. I could never visit enough sick people. I could never connect with my volunteers enough. I could never get ahead of the pace of Sunday coming after Sunday after Sunday. There was always more to do, and there were always people waiting on me for something seemingly important. And I know I wasn't the only one who struggled. Having staff on stress leave was a regular occurrence in our team.

In my employment contract, there was allocated time for reading and training and an allowance to take four additional Sundays off a year to compensate for having to work every weekend. I also had sick leave entitlements. On paper, it was fair and reasonable. But in reality, I rarely took the time off I was entitled to. There was simply too much to do.

And it wasn't my employer's fault. I don't blame them at all. It was on me.

It's not just in the church world; the corporate sector these days is just as pressured. My husband worked in the computing industry, and his evenings and weekends were always busy with new technology to learn, his days pressured by sales targets to meet and clients to serve. I have close friends and family members in the education and healthcare sectors who are under enormous and relentless pressure. Busy doesn't begin to describe how much they need to get done each day to barely keep up with demand.

It's out of control. The demands of modern life are destroying us. Is this really the way God wants us to live? Is nonstop busyness honouring to God? Or are we carrying a burden Jesus never laid on us to carry?

***

I remember once wasting hours in an airport. We were booked on an early flight to Sydney. Murray had a training seminar to attend, and we decided to make his one-day business trip into a weekend getaway for two. But when we arrived at the airport, it was blanketed in thick fog, and we weren't going anywhere anytime soon.

We had to wait.

We had to wait for hours and hours. We ordered an overpriced coffee and sat, staring at the fog out of the floor-to-ceiling windows.

It was uncomfortable, sitting with nowhere to go and nothing to do but stare and think. At first, I got out my phone to try to answer some emails and do some reading, but soon I took a hint from the Spirit and allowed myself to simply be still.

Take a deep breath. Be still.

Or, as we read in the Psalms, selah.

I love where my mind goes when I sit still for a while. When I'm not weighed down by worry or guilt and take time to be still, my mind goes to a creative place. This is when I have my best ideas. This is when I solve problems. This is when I have ideas for my writing, I think up gift ideas for my kids' Christmas lists, think of places I'd love to go and new things I'd like to try. This is where I dream.

I have a friend who published her first book a couple of years ago. It is fun and insightful, a great read. She has a lovely conversational writing style that makes you feel like you're having coffee with your best friend as you read. I was standing with her while someone asked when she was going to write her next book (we all know she has many more in her). She answered, "I'm too busy. I only get creative when I'm bored."

I've never forgotten that sentence.

"I only get creative when I'm bored."

It wasn't a lack of time or will. It was the mental clutter and pace of productivity that kept her from writing. She is smart and capable, a high achiever, and too busy to be bored.

Time spent sitting still, allowing ourselves to be bored, can be very uncomfortable. Our minds and bodies are unaccustomed to stillness. We are so used to being preoccupied and distracted.

Technology has changed the way we live. With the invention of the personal computer, the internet, email, and the mobile phone, our minds are on call 24/7, literally. There is nowhere we can go to get away from the office. We can't avoid being informed and in touch. We are constantly bombarded with more information, more news, and more demands.

For many of us, the way we disconnect from work demands is to distract ourselves with more technology and information. We binge-watch Netflix, listen to podcasts, watch YouTube, and scroll Instagram. Our minds never get to rest. Our minds never get to unwind. And our thoughts, feelings and emotions never get a chance to be processed.

When I first started practising stillness in the days after my hospital stay, I dreaded the silence. Not only was stillness uncomfortable, but the thoughts and memories that came to mind were unpleasant. My thoughts were full of what I thought I should have done differently. I should have trained more volunteers and delegated more tasks. I should have said no to more unreasonable demands. I should have been more organised. I should have been home more for my kids. I should have been better.

I was hurt. I was disappointed. I had so many regrets and didn't want to think about them. I wanted to be distracted.

My counsellor invited me to sit in silence, comfortable, eyes closed, and imagine myself in a pleasant place, and then to invite Jesus to sit with me. As the thoughts and feelings came into my mind, I talked them over with Jesus. I confessed my sin and asked for forgiveness. I received comfort and encouragement. I felt all the feelings. I cried the tears. I relived the memories. I gave my burdens to Jesus, and I began to heal. Slowly, I began to recognise God's hand in the hard moments of my story. He was there with me in my hurt, and He was with me in my healing. But it took time and courage to sit quietly and allow my mind to go to the places I had been avoiding in my pain.

Author and teacher John Mark Comer describes his experience of quiet and solitude in a similar way:

> *We start to feel. At first we feel the whole gamut of human emotions—not just joy and gratitude and celebration and restfulness but also sadness and doubt and anger and anxiety. Usually I feel all the lousy emotions first. That's just how it goes.*[11]

I wasn't very good at stillness. I was advised to have four weeks off work to recover. I took less than two. There was too much to do. I was too busy to take time off work. And, by this stage, I was well-practised at pushing through.

There were a lot of reasons why I didn't take extended time off. I didn't feel sick enough. I didn't want to let people down and I didn't want to add extra pressure to my busy colleagues. Why was it so hard to slow down and allow clear space in my calendar? Why was I so uncomfortable with taking time to rest and heal?

Perhaps John Mark Comer hit the nail on the head when he said, "Hurry is a form of violence on the soul."[12] Our hearts are constantly in recovery from the unrelenting pace of our busy lives.

***

What does Jesus think about our busyness? There are a few things I find interesting about Jesus' ministry that can help us understand how to unburden from our busyness.

Jesus had a practice of spending time in solitude, even during the busiest times of ministry. In Mark chapter one, right at the beginning of Jesus' ministry, He was gaining popularity and under pressure to do more. Verse 33 tells us, "The whole town gathered at the door." Jesus had been teaching in the synagogue and healing the sick and demon-possessed. The following morning, Mark tells us, "While it was still dark, Jesus got up, left the house and went off to a solitary place, where he prayed."[13]

Jesus was busy; people were looking for His help, but He couldn't be found. He was off on His own, spending time in solitude.

While it was common for Jesus to pray early in the morning before the day began, sometimes He took time out in the middle of the day. Matthew 13:1 says, "That same day Jesus went out of the house and sat by the lake."

Jesus, the Saviour of the world, sitting by the water in the middle of the day.

Now that's countercultural. By today's standards, that's just plain irresponsible.

Jesus set His own agenda. He invested time in solitude with His Father, and He followed His own schedule.

I have completely underestimated the importance and impact of quiet solitude as a self-care or spiritual discipline. We live in such a noisy world. Being alone with God and our thoughts almost never happens unless we are very intentional about practising it. But, when we get there, when we carve out the time and create the environment, it changes us.

Another thing that surprises me about Jesus is how much of His ministry is conducted in the interruptions, on the sidelines. Jesus seemed to always have time to be interrupted. The woman healed from her bleeding, Jesus' healing of blind Bartimaeus, healing the ten blind men, the lepers, blessing the little children. The list goes on. Jesus always had time for interruptions. I didn't.

I have one vivid memory from when my children were small. Having three children close together in age wasn't carefully thought through. It took us a while to fall pregnant with our first child, so we assumed number two would be similar. I fell pregnant straight away and our first two babies were born seventeen months apart. Number three arrived two years later, giving me three children under three and a half. I was a full-time stay-at-home mum, just trying to keep us all fed, watered, and with at least one set of clean clothes somewhere in the laundry rotation.

As busy as I was with day-to-day childcare, I wanted to stay involved in church, so I volunteered to help organise creative elements for our Sunday services, something I was passionate about and loved.

"Not now, darling, Mummy's busy."

The baby was asleep, and the toddler was quietly entertaining herself. These were precious moments to finally get something done, but the three-year-old wanted attention.

"Not now, darling, Mummy's busy."

I don't know how many times I said this sentence out loud. Somehow, God finally broke through my dogged focus and opened my eyes to my number one mission field. I resigned from my position on the creative team for a season to focus on my young family.

If Jesus had time to be interrupted, we should too. And if we are too busy to notice and give our attention to those interruptions, we need to reassess our schedules.

***

I often read the gospels through the lens of my twenty-first-century life. I read the stories of Jesus' encounters with the people He ministered to, preaching, healing, teaching His disciples, and confronting the Pharisees, and I imagine each event lined up neatly in a Google calendar in half-hour time allocations. In my ignorance, I fail to understand the pace of Jesus' ministry.

It wasn't until I read John Eldredge's book *Get Your Life Back* that I even considered the speed of Jesus' life and ministry. Jesus wasn't dashing from one appointment to the next, one eye on the clock, impatient to move on.

When we read, "The next day Jesus decided to leave for Galilee"[14], we don't realise that the next destination is a three-day walk away. Three days.

Jesus moved at walking pace. He spent time outside enjoying the wide-open sky and beautiful landscape. There were hours spent chatting with His disciples, thinking, and getting ideas for His parables and sermon illustrations. He spent hours in prayer with His Heavenly Father. Much of Jesus' ministry was slow.

Sure, Jesus had crowds of people following Him, wanting something from Him. There were times when His life was in danger. No doubt, He encountered bad weather, hunger, and thirst. There were times when Jesus had a lot to do. But the impression I get from reading the gospels is that Jesus' ministry wasn't hurried.

What would it look like for us to not be in a hurry all the

time? Can you imagine it? What if there was a different way to live, unburdened by busyness?

Our loving God gave us a rhythm of rest and work to follow from the very beginning of creation.

> *By the seventh day God had finished the work he had been doing; so on the seventh day he rested from all his work. Then God blessed the seventh day and made it holy, because on it he rested from all the work of creating that he had done.*[15]

Before Adam and Eve worked one day in the garden, they enjoyed a day of rest to connect with each other, with their Creator God, and enjoy the beauty of their home. We were not designed to work seven days a week. God does not expect us to work to the point of exhaustion and burnout. He invites us to rest.

The word Sabbath simply means to stop. Stop working. Take time off from striving to make a living; take time to rest and worship. Not just occasionally, but every week. One whole day, every single week. That's Sabbath.

After the Children of Israel had been slaves in Egypt for hundreds of years and God rescued them, bringing them to the Promised Land to become His people once again, God gave Moses the Law. He gave the people a set of laws that taught them how to live and how to be in relationship with a holy God. The Law is summarised in the Ten Commandments. Number four is to keep the Sabbath.

> *Remember the Sabbath day by keeping it holy. Six days you shall labor and do all your work, but the seventh day is a sabbath to the Lord your God. On it you shall not do any work, neither you, nor your son or daughter, nor your male or female servant, nor your animals, nor any*

foreigner residing in your towns. For in six days the Lord made the heavens and the earth, the sea, and all that is in them, but he rested on the seventh day. Therefore the Lord blessed the Sabbath day and made it holy.[16]

When the people were slaves, they didn't enjoy days off. No doubt, they worked seven days a week, every day of the year. Their time was not their own. So when God gave the people His Law, He reminded them to take a day off each week to rest. And God extends the same invitation to us in our 24/7 modern world.

The Sabbath is not something to be legalistic about. Jesus got in trouble with the religious leaders for not following the Sabbath properly. Jesus healed people on the Sabbath day, which was against their rules. It was scandalous! But Jesus knew, "The Sabbath was made for man, not man for the Sabbath."[17]

God gifted us the Sabbath day because it is good for us. He knows we need rest. He knows we need to disconnect from the demands of the world and re-focus our attention on Him. God knows we need to refill our energy, reconnect with one another, and spend time in worship.

The biblical Sabbath began at sunset on Friday evening with a special family meal—a celebration. Then, Saturday was a day of rest and worship. The Sabbath ended at sunset on Saturday, and preparations began for the busy week ahead.

Christians today tend to practise Sabbath on Sunday, because Jesus rose on the first day of the week and the early church celebrated that. We could have a theological debate about what day of the week you should rest, but that's not the point. The bottom line is that we take time away from our work each week to rest.

When I was growing up in a small town, Sundays were

very quiet. We spent the morning at church, came home for a family lunch and a long nap, and were back at church in the evening. This is a lovely rhythm, but it's not always realistic. There are many people who don't get to have the day off on Sundays. And when you work in the church, Sunday is the busiest day of the week.

What might keeping the Sabbath look like for us today? How can we honour God's design for our lives without creating legalistic rules?

We've lived all of our married lives in Brisbane, the capital city of our state. Brisbane is like any other city. It doesn't stop. The shops are open seven days a week. Our local supermarket is open from 6 am until 9 pm every day. The shops are busiest on the weekends.

Imagine our surprise when we were in outback Queensland and went into town to grab a few supplies for dinner, and all the shops were shut. All of them. The supermarket was shut. The bakery and pharmacy were closed. The only things open in the whole town were the pub and the service station. We could buy fuel and beer—that's it. From noon Saturday until Monday morning, the whole town stopped.

It took us some time to get used to the idea of planning our week around the shop's opening hours, but after a while, we learned to love the peace of weekends in the outback. Everything was quiet. Everyone was at home. What a gift.

The Sabbath looks different in each season of life. When we have small children, we can't simply take a day off—their needs have to be met. But there are some things we can do to clear space in a day and take time to rest. We can have a day where we eat leftovers or takeaway. We can pause our cleaning and laundry schedule. We can organise our week so we have a day when we don't need to go to the shops or show up to meetings. We can turn off our notifications and leave the computer in its bag. We can protect time in the calendar to do the things that refresh our souls and reconnect us with God and each other.

Attending a church service and participating in corporate worship is an important spiritual practice, but it is not the only way to worship God. I enjoy God's presence in the beauty of creation, in private Bible study and sitting around the dinner table with friends and family. And, as an introvert, church services often leave me feeling drained. I love it, but I come home wanting to withdraw rather than connect. So time spent in solitude is important for my spiritual well-being.

My perfect Sabbath begins with dinner with my husband, or even better, my whole family on Friday evening. Then Saturday morning is slow. I may take my journal to a local cafe or walk to the farmers market to buy myself a bunch of fresh flowers. We go to a local restaurant for a poke bowl for lunch, full of fresh healthy vegetables. Then, I spend the afternoon reading, knitting and taking a nap. I cook something simple for Saturday dinner, and we may watch a movie before bed. By Sunday morning I feel rested and ready for another week.

What might a Sabbath day look like for you?

God didn't intend for me to spend my life rushing from one thing to the next. Being in a constant hurry isn't honouring to Him. He doesn't expect me to work 24/7 or jump at the beck and call of everyone. God wants me to slow down, to have time for interruptions, to spend time resting each week, and to allow my mind to wander, dream and process.

I saw a quote by author Wanda E. Brunstetter on social media recently that said, "If you are too busy to pray, then you are busier than God wants you to be."[18] Motivational speaker Matthew Kelly says, "If you don't have time to pray and read the Scriptures, you are busier than God ever intended you to be."[19] I would add that if you don't have time to be still in solitude, if you don't have time to be interrupted and take a day off work, then you are doing more than God wants.

When we returned from our trip around the country I got a tattoo. It's either very modern or very silly of me, but anyway, I did it. It is the word 'selah', the Hebrew word we find in the Psalms to indicate an interlude, a pause. It's written in a pretty script across my wrist. It is a constant reminder to stop and reflect, to slow down and lean into the interruptions, to notice what God is doing in my life and in my world.

TAKE TIME TO REFLECT

- ☼ Are you too busy? Do you spend your days hurrying from one commitment to the next? Do you feel frustrated when you are interrupted because you know it will put you behind?

- ☼ Do you have a regular time to stop work and rest? Is there a time in your week when you can sit in silence and solitude? Do you have a regular rhythm of rest and worship?

Here are some practical steps to lay this burden down:

- Spend ten minutes in silent solitude. Turn off all distractions and sit with God.

- Build some margin into your calendar to allow for interruptions.

- Plan a Sabbath day. Clear your schedule, get the shopping and cooking done ahead of time, and take a day off to rest and worship. Notice how it makes you feel.

- Set aside time each day to close your computer, turn off all notifications, and be fully present.

4

GIRLS CAN DO ANYTHING

THE BURDEN OF UNREALISTIC EXPECTATIONS

"What church are you from?"

I was milling around in the foyer, coffee in hand, waiting for the church planting conference to begin. Our church was hosting the conference. There were multiple denominations from the area on site for the two-day event. I was trying to be friendly, chatting to unfamiliar faces.

"I'm from here," I answered.

"Oh, you must have answered the phone when we registered," the visitor said.

"No, I don't work in the office. That would have been Glenys," I replied.

"So you're here to prepare the morning tea then?"

I wish I could have recorded the look on his face when I told him I was the Discipleship Pastor of this, one of the largest Baptist churches in the country. It was a look of confusion and surprise. Perhaps he had never met a female pastor before. The conversation didn't get much further before he found someone else he needed to urgently catch up with.

I am so blessed to be able to follow God's call on my life into pastoral ministry. I know that in many places, my vocation would not be possible. In many churches, women answer the phone and prepare morning tea. But things are changing, and doors are opening for women.

In 1966, Australian law changed to allow married women to work in the public service. While this opened the door for women to continue in their jobs as teachers, nurses and secretaries after marriage, many companies didn't change their policies until much later. Until then, when a woman married, she had to give up her career and become a full-time homemaker. There were very few choices; the pathway was clear. Once married, a woman's place was in the home. Her days consisted of cooking, cleaning and caring for children. This was normal, and there were very few exceptions.

Oh, how things have changed in a few short generations. The door is now open for women in almost all areas of the workplace. In some professions it is still difficult; there are cultural barriers, and the gender pay gap is still a very real problem. But we now see women following their dreams and using their gifts in all spheres of professional life.

Girls can do anything. I have loved seeing the explosion of women's sports here in Australia in recent years. The women's rugby league, Australian football, soccer, and cricket teams are filling stadiums around the country. There are women on the front lines of our defence forces, police force, paramedic and firefighting crews. They are highly trained, highly skilled, and highly valued. Women are bringing their gifts and skills to the Australian workforce, and the traditional role of womanhood is being redefined.

These opportunities to follow our dreams and contribute to the family income have become easier than ever before with the availability of great childcare options for young mums. Paid maternity leave is available to many women who choose to have children, allowing them to return to their position after spending time at home when their children are born. Our generation is overcoming many of the obstacles that previously prevented women from staying in the workforce.

More recently I've noticed many women starting their own businesses. With the opportunities the internet provides for global connectedness and platform, women are selling their skills and products online from kitchen tables and garages around the world, toddlers underfoot. Women entrepreneurs are taking over the small business world, and it's exciting to be part of it.

All of this is very good. I think our Heavenly Father looks down and smiles at His daughters growing in stature and influence. We bring an important voice and perspective to every room we walk into. But a problem arises when the opportunities we have available to us become expectations that weigh heavy on us.

Just because we can, doesn't mean we should. But often, that's how it feels.

In our Pinterest-perfect, Instagram-following world,

opportunities can feel like expectations. Things we could do, become things we think we should do. There is an unwritten expectation. There is a pull to go with the flow.

You should be back at work as soon as possible after having your babies.

You should start a business.

You should go for that promotion, work overtime, and get another degree.

The opportunities that are available, thanks to generations who fought for changes in our workplaces and education systems, have opened up a new world to modern women. But it can be hard to look at the smorgasbord of opportunities and not feel the pressure to take hold of every single one. It's hard to say 'no' when the world is chanting, 'go'. Women are no longer stuck at home; we are now so busy we never get home.

I was a schoolteacher when I fell pregnant with our first child. The expectation was that I would take the twelve weeks available leave and then return to my position. When I resigned instead, I had several concerned colleagues counsel me to reconsider. I was throwing my career away. I would regret becoming a full-time mother. I was going backward.

Deciding to be a stay-at-home mother was like swimming upstream. It was a decision that challenged the expectations of the professional women around me who worked hard to become teachers.

But I did stay home, for thirteen beautiful years, eventually returning to part-time teaching in the school my children attended. Then, I got a phone call from my pastor. He asked me to fill in for a staff member who had to leave ministry suddenly. It was supposed to be just three days a week for three months while the church looked for a new candidate.

I worked in pastoral ministry for over ten years. I already had a Bachelor of Education, so I went to Bible college for a graduate certificate to qualify for ministry. But, as a woman, I could not qualify for ordination in my denomination, so I stopped studying. I love learning, but studying is very expensive, time-consuming and stressful. I have friends in ministry who persevered and gained their master's, but that wasn't the right choice for me.

Just a few weeks ago, at our annual business assembly, my denomination voted to change the rules, allowing women to be ordained. For a few short minutes, I wondered what this meant for me. Should I get back on board the train to gain the highest qualification I can? Should I climb to the top of the ladder that has just opened up for women like me? There is part of me that wants to go for it, just to make a point. But no. This open door is not for me to walk through. There are young, gifted pastors with a ministry call from God on their lives who will be recognised and affirmed by this change, and I will do everything I can to encourage them and cheer them on. But it's not for me. Just because I can, doesn't mean I should.

**

Do you feel the weight of expectations? Do you ever feel like you should be doing more?

There is an expectation from our culture to be involved in the workforce and push boundaries in that realm, but there is also an expectation as Christian women that we should do certain things and be a certain way.

The Proverbs 31 woman is the Superwoman of Christian femininity. Like Mary Poppins, she is practically perfect in every way. When I read about her vigorous work, her lamp that doesn't go out and her household dressed in scarlet, she makes me feel more tired than inspired. Proverbs 31 gives us a long list of expectations to live up to as a woman who is trying to live a godly life.

But this isn't the intention of this scripture. Proverbs 31 is not a description of the perfect Christian woman for us all to copy. Let's take a fresh look at this familiar passage.

At the beginning of the chapter, we read that Proverbs 31 was a poem taught to a young King named Lemuel by his mother. It is an acrostic poem, each line beginning with successive letters of the Hebrew alphabet.

The chapter begins with instructions for a king to be sober and wise, to rule fairly and without partiality. And it continues to describe the qualities of a prospective wife, someone of great value to the king. The poem is not a detailed description of a particular woman. The Proverbs 31 woman didn't literally exist. The qualities described in the poem are a celebration of the qualities a wise young man should look for in a wife—a wife worth more than rubies (v10); a wife who brings him good all the days of her life (v12). The poem describes the hopes and dreams of a mother for her son as he chooses a life partner.

I wholeheartedly empathise with this mother. I have a son who is engaged to be married. For many years he watched as his friends went through a succession of girlfriends while he waited. Eventually, he found the one. She is a smart, hard-working, godly young woman—the kind of woman described in Proverbs 31.

As it turns out, King Lemuel's mother was a wise woman! Her advice to a young man looking for a wife is spot on.

I love the conclusion to the poem.

> *Charm is deceptive, and beauty is fleeting; but a woman who fears the Lord is to be praised.*[20]

That sums it up perfectly. This is the message I want for my son. Choose a wife, not for her charm or beauty, but for her character, her love for God, her heart.

When we read through the qualities of the wife described in Proverbs 31 in light of the role of women in the culture of the time, it is quite astounding. Women were not valued. They couldn't testify in a court of law; they had few legal rights and enjoyed very little personal freedom. And yet, the Proverbs 31 woman is an entrepreneur and profitable business owner. She is smart and strong; she manages her household with excellence; she is generous, wise and honoured. She is highly valued.

If you do a little research into Jewish family tradition, you will find that the male head of Jewish households sang the Proverbs 31 poem over their wife as a blessing on Friday evenings as the family gathered to celebrate the Sabbath meal. It is a blessing, a celebration, a poem of honour and value.

And yet, when we read this chapter of Scripture and try to apply it to our lives, we can feel inadequate. We feel like a failure because we don't live up to the list. Instead of feeling celebrated and honoured, we feel overwhelmed and pressured. Instead of feeling empowered, we feel trapped. Instead of feeling accomplished, we feel an expectation to perform and achieve.

The truth is, most women I know are living Proverbs 31 lives and could stand proudly before King Lemuel's mother any day of the week. They are smart and strong; they work hard raising their kids, loving their husbands, and managing their homes, often while working or building businesses as well. They are capable, independent, wise, generous, and kind.

Yes, I'm talking about you. You are capable, independent, wise, generous and kind.

This doesn't just apply to married women and mothers. I know single women who are godly and generous, setting an example to those in their sphere of influence. I know women with mental illness who courageously fight for health and strength every day. I know women who don't fit the neat square mould, and yet they embody the qualities and character of the godly woman Proverbs 31 describes.

This passage of the Bible shouldn't weigh us down, rather, it should set us free. God created women to be strong and capable, honourable and highly valued. And that is what we are.

So, then, how do we decipher the bombardment of expectations coming from all directions? How do we know who to be and what to do with our lives? How do we know what God actually expects? There are a few key verses that can serve as guideposts to help us.

Keep it Simple – Micah 6:8

The leaders of Israel were outwardly going through the motions of religious piety, but also unjustly exploiting the poor and vulnerable for their own advantage. The rich were paying off phoney prophets to preach messages in their favour. And God was angry. He sent Micah to warn the leaders of the coming judgement. But, along with words of warning were words of hope.

One of the most familiar verses in the book of Micah is this:

> *He has shown you, O mortal, what is good. And what does the Lord require of you? To act justly and to love mercy and to walk humbly with your God.*[21]

So often we overcomplicate things. It is in our nature. But

Micah reminds us to keep it simple. God has shown us what is good, so just do that.

Act justly: don't lie, cheat and steal. Don't take advantage of people. Do the right thing.

Love mercy: be kind and generous to those in need, forgive people who hurt you, give people the benefit of the doubt.

And walk humbly with God: walk each day in relationship with your Saviour, in step with Jesus. Not to seek fame and fortune, but to bring glory and honour to Him.

Do Good – Ephesians 2:10

The Apostle Paul tells us:

For we are God's handiwork, created in Christ Jesus to do good works, which God prepared in advance for us to do.[22]

God created each one of us uniquely. He has given us gifts, talents, passions, and dreams and He expects us to use them. Do the things only you can do. Only you can love your husband and raise your children if you have them, so make that a priority. Do the things that light you up; feed your passion and make the most of your strengths. Only you have your unique mix of gifts and passions, and we each need to take responsibility for what God calls us to do.

Love God and Others – Luke 10:27

'Love the Lord your God with all your heart and with all your soul and with all your strength and with all your mind'; and, 'Love your neighbour as yourself.'[23]

The bottom line is always love. Love God and love each

other. Will striving for a promotion at work help you to love God more? Then go for it with all your heart. If not, don't feel obliged. Is volunteering to serve morning tea to the mothers group at church an act of love for you? Then make it the very best morning tea you are capable of. But, if volunteering for the mothers group makes you stressed and cranky when you get home, then you are not loving the people only you can love, and it probably isn't a good investment of your time.

So, out of all the opportunities available to women today, what does God expect?

It has been interesting in this season of my life how I have had to fight off the temptation to do more. I have more freedom and opportunity right now than I have ever had in my life. We are financially secure, and I don't need to work simply for the income. My children are all grown and don't require my time and attention. My home is small and simple, so I don't have a lot of housework to do. I have freedom. I have time.

When there is a call at church to cook meals for the homeless on Thursdays, I ask God if that is for me. When I see ministry opportunities, job vacancies and training courses, I ask God if it is for me. Sometimes He says yes. But often, He says no. I don't need to do everything, filling my calendar and pushing to the max. I have discovered permission to do my part, and nothing more—because the opportunities I am involved in are so much sweeter when I have the time and energy to put my whole heart into them.

Our pastor asked me to preach a few weeks ago. I hadn't preached a sermon in a regular church service for quite a while, and I wanted to do the best I could. Usually, I have had to squeeze sermon preparation in between regular meetings and work commitments, so it was wonderful to have headspace and time to prepare properly. Saying no to some things makes the yeses so much better.

How can we manage expectations? How can we examine the expectations we put on ourselves of how much we should do? How do we discern what God has planned for us? Remember our key verse, Matthew 11:28-30. Jesus tells us His yoke is easy and His burden is *light*. If you are feeling weighed down by the expectations you have of yourself, your workplace, your church or your family, it's time to re-examine those expectations.

TAKE TIME TO REFLECT

☼ Do you feel like you should be doing more? Do you feel obliged to chase after every opportunity for self-improvement and advancement? Do you feel like your contribution is never enough?

☼ Are you concerned that you are not fulfilling your full potential? Do you struggle to discern God's plan for your life?

Here are some practical steps to lay this burden down:

- List the things in your life that only you can do. Add the things you are passionate about—the things that light you up and fill you with joy.

- Identify the things in your life that you would describe as obligations—things you do simply because they seem normal or expected.

- Make a 'not-to-do' list and practise saying no to extra obligations and opportunities.

- Ask God to help you set your priorities in this season of your life.

5

PENNY FOR YOUR THOUGHTS

THE BURDEN OF WORRY

"How are you?"

I slipped into the back row of the church next to an old friend I hadn't seen for a while, waiting for the prayer meeting to begin.

She was one of two teacher aides in her school, and they had been told that one of the positions would be made redundant at the end of the year. There was a fifty-fifty chance that she would lose her job in a few short months. And she was worried.

Really worried.

She explained to me that she hadn't been eating or sleeping and was suffering from chronic nausea. She was literally worried sick. The possibility of her job loss was all she could think about, day and night.

I understand. She had every reason to be worried. Who wouldn't worry in this situation?

A few years ago, I found a lump in my breast. I was in my mid-forties with three teenage children. My maternal grandmother died of breast cancer when she was only forty-two, and I have multiple aunts and cousins who have gone through treatment. It's in my family, and I thought it was my turn.

I went to my doctor, who sent me for a mammogram and biopsy. There were a couple of weeks between when I first found the lump and when I got the phone call to tell me everything was normal. It was just a cyst. Those weeks were long. Each day was long, and the nights longer. The way Murray and I looked at each other was full of concern and fear. I cried a lot in those weeks. I prayed a lot.

But mostly, I worried.

***

I tend to worry about things that are out of my control. I worry about my kids' jobs. I worry about my daughter's stress levels. I worry about rents going up in my children's apartment buildings. All of the worry about my kids is unnecessary. They are all grown adults. They are all making good choices, have stable jobs and have lived in the same places for years now. They do not benefit from my worrying about them. Nor do I.

I don't only worry about things that are out of my control.

I also replay things that happened to me over and over in my head. I replay conversations and comments, embarrassing moments and awkward interactions. Over and over and over again, they replay in my head, stuck on repeat.

Looking back over my life now, I feel like I've lost a lot of years to stress and worry. I'm very good at stressing. I was a stressed mum. I was a stressed wife. I was a stressed pastor. I was very good at hiding it and appearing calm on the outside, but I was like a duck, paddling for my life underwater where no one could see.

Life is hard. There are a lot of balls to juggle. There is a constant onslaught of demands and pressures. And our minds gradually get worn down with the pace of it all. Like a frog in a slowly simmering pot, soon our world reaches boiling point, but it feels normal for us. We've forgotten what the cool pond feels like. We didn't notice the temperature slowly rising.

Being stressed out is normal. The prevalence of anxiety and stress-related illness is reaching epidemic levels. According to an Australian National Study of Mental Health and Wellbeing conducted in 2020–2021, 3.4 million Australians aged 16–85 years, that's 17% of our adult population, saw a health professional for their mental health.

Being calm and at peace is definitely not the norm. The COVID-19 pandemic boosted the stress levels of the world, and they haven't returned to normal.

The thing we don't always realise about worrying is that we are in control. We get to choose. I love the way Max Lucado explains it:

> You can be the air traffic controller of your mental airport. You occupy the control tower and can direct the mental traffic of your world. Thoughts circle above,

> *coming and going. If one of them lands, it is because you gave it permission. If it leaves, it is because you directed it to do so. You can select your thought pattern.*[24]

What's it like inside your head? Is it a calm and pleasant place to be? Is it encouraging, affirming and inspiring? Or is it a scary place? What does the voice in your head say to you all day?

Our thoughts are so important. What we think about matters. We need to curate the voice in our heads because we usually, eventually, believe what it tells us. And we are the only ones who can hear it, tell it to be quiet, or change the narrative.

Part of the reason we distract ourselves with TV, podcasts, music and radio, rather than keep our homes quiet, is to help us avoid thinking our thoughts. Because often, our thoughts are not kind. We are mean to ourselves. We are critical, disappointed, worried and anxious. Our minds are not calm or happy places to hang out and spend time.

I'm not implying that we can cure the world's anxiety by thinking positive thoughts; I understand the mental health crisis is more complex. But we can make a huge difference by learning to trust God's Word and meditating on His truths to guide the way we think.

The words we have running around in our heads impact the way we live our lives. They impact the way we feel, the way we perform and what we can achieve. I listened to a podcast one day about a runner. At the time, I was trying to improve my fitness and had tried running, but I hated it. I only lasted about a hundred metres, and I found myself gasping for air, my heart beating out of my chest. I discovered, over time, that if I pushed through the discomfort and kept going, soon my breathing and heart rate would stabilise, and I would be able to keep running. But there was an uncomfortable barrier I had to push through every time.

The guy on the podcast described how he ran a marathon by repeating this simple sentence to himself: "I am a good runner; running is easy." These were the words he said to himself, over and over again. "I am a good runner; running is easy."

I thought I'd give it a try.

Off I went, "I'm a good runner; running is easy." As I struggled to breathe, "I'm a good runner; running is easy." As my heart rate began to peak, "I'm a good runner; running is easy." As I found my stride, "I'm a good runner; running is easy." Over and over, I told myself, "I'm a good runner; running is easy."

And you know what? It worked! My running improved, and the initial discomfort to get myself moving lessened over time. It felt good to affirm myself for doing something hard and taking care of my health instead of thinking, "This is stupid, you look stupid, this is so hard, I hate running." Affirming myself and cheering myself on improved my attitude and my performance.

The words in our heads, our thoughts and attitudes, rule our lives. Our worrying thoughts can make us physically sick. They can make us angry and say things we don't mean. They can steal our peace, keeping us awake at night. And they make us selfish. It is hard to see the look of hurt in another's eyes when we are completely occupied with our own problems. Worry makes our world small.

No wonder the Apostle Paul tells us to take captive every thought and make it obedient to Christ.[25] It is a spiritual discipline, an act of faith. Because as hard as it may be, we can control our thoughts. We can choose what to think about. It's up to us.

One of the most powerful tools I have found to take captive my thoughts of worry is to recite Scripture I've memorised. As a little girl I attended AWANA, a Friday night youth club at church. Part of every program was Scripture memorisation. We had little books of verses to learn by heart to earn badges for our uniforms. I wasn't very good at it. I found it difficult and frustrating. But I can still remember the verses I memorised more than forty years ago.

Many days as I was driving to work, knowing I had a difficult meeting or an overcrowded to-do list waiting for me, I would recite out loud, "Trust in the Lord with all your heart and lean not on your own understanding; in all your ways submit to him, and he will make your paths straight."[26]

Repeating those words lifted my thoughts from my own inadequacy to God's sufficiency. The words captured my thoughts of worry and fear and boosted my faith.

One of the first big adventures we tackled on our travels was a beautiful sand island called K'gari. It is only accessible by four-wheel drive, and we were novices. The tracks were narrow and bumpy, and when a car was approaching from the other direction it was tricky to get out of the way of each other. I was a nervous wreck. I was not having fun.

Have you ever chosen a word of the year? It's become a popular thing with several of the social media personalities I follow. Usually, the word I choose has little impact on my year, but that year, my word was courage, and it was based on Joshua 1:9.

> *Have I not commanded you? Be strong and courageous. Do not be afraid; do not be discouraged, for the Lord your God will be with you wherever you go.*

I learned the verse while I was teaching it to children at church. I made up actions and a song to help the children remember the words. And, of course, it stuck in my head too. So, as we adventured around K'gari, I found myself repeating the familiar instructions from God. "Be strong and courageous. Don't be afraid; don't be discouraged." And God's truth dispelled my fear and helped me to find peace in a stressful situation.

***

In the Sermon on the Mount, Jesus devotes a whole section to worry. In summary, He says, don't worry about anything. God knows what you need, and He will look after you. More specifically, He says, don't worry about what you will eat or what you will wear. Don't worry about food and clothes. My, didn't Jesus knock the nail on the head with that one? How much time have I wasted in my life thinking about what to wear to work and what to eat for dinner? As mothers, isn't half our life spent in the laundry and the kitchen? Jesus, I feel seen.

How often do you hear, "Mum, what's for dinner?" How often are you asked, "Mum, where are my shoes? Are there any clean socks?" Jesus knew. He considers it all and tells us, "Don't worry."

Simple? Yes. Easy? No. Not easy at all. Because worry is so normal, it feels irresponsible not to worry about our everyday needs. How are we going to get by unless we worry about it? But Jesus says, no, I've got you, trust me.

Don't worry. Trust me.

There is a particular Bible story that is one of my favourites. It is so normal, I can imagine myself in the room. Perhaps you can too. Jesus and His disciples were visiting His friends in Bethany; Mary, Martha and Lazarus. Martha was busy in the kitchen preparing a meal for her guests. Mary, on the other hand, was sitting on the floor in the living room, listening to Jesus teaching His disciples as if she were a disciple herself.

This got up Martha's nose. It wasn't fair. The workload was too much for her. Mary wasn't doing what she should be doing—helping in the kitchen.

Eventually, Martha went in and interrupted Jesus. "Tell Mary to come and help me." But she didn't like Jesus' answer.

> "Martha, Martha," the Lord answered, "you are worried and upset about many things, but few things are needed—or indeed only one. Mary has chosen what is better, and it will not be taken away from her."[27]

Jesus called out Martha's attitude—you are worried and upset. Can you relate to this as much as I can?

I could put up with a reasonable amount of mess around the house, especially when the children were young. Keeping our home tidy was a challenge. There was always a pile of laundry somewhere, toys out and about, dishes on the kitchen bench and toothpaste on the bathroom sink.

But, although our home had a lived-in messy feel, when we were expecting guests, I went into full impress mode. I turned into a dragon mother cleaning freak. I yelled. I yelled a lot. I angrily scooped up toys, washed dishes, folded laundry and wiped up spills. It wasn't pretty.

One particular extended family member would notice my mess and their critique of my housekeeping abilities was hurtful. Their comments would stick and replay in my mind. But that didn't justify my behaviour towards my young family in the hour leading up to their visits. My behaviour was driven by pride. It was not God-honouring. I can see that now.

I wish Jesus had walked in and said, "Christine, Christine,

you are worried and upset about many things, but this doesn't matter." I wish He had come and told me to leave the dishes, take a deep breath, and come sit and chat, to spend time sitting at His feet, refocusing my heart on what was truly important.

A few weeks ago, some old friends invited us around for dinner. We hadn't seen them for years and the invitation came out of the blue. They lit a firepit in the backyard and we spent hours catching up on the news of lost time. You'll never guess what they served for dinner. Frozen pizza. Yes, we ate store-bought pizza, out of the freezer and straight into the oven. It was the best night simply because our hosts had the Mary and Martha paradigm spot-on. Their hospitality was all about relationship and connection and not at all about being impressive. There was no stress, just good conversation. And the pizza tasted pretty good too.

But what about the big things? Jesus can tell us not to worry about simple things like what to wear and what to eat and prioritising relationships over impressive hospitality, but what about when life crashes in around us, and hospitality is the last thing on our minds?

What about when the diagnosis is not benign? When our children are not doing well, we lose our homes, lose our marriages, or lose someone we love. Are the restless nights filled with worry warranted when we are the one who loses our job? How do we avoid getting caught in a cycle of worry when the stakes are high and the danger is real? Isn't worry inevitable? Can we trust God when life truly falls to pieces?

This is a great question, and this is where looking at examples from the Bible is so helpful. Because there are many, many examples of people whose lives fell apart, and God was still faithful. We can read about what happened to them, we can read what God said, and what God did. And bit by bit, we can learn to trust our God who is the same today as He was back then.

One day, Jesus and His disciples were on a boat crossing the Sea of Galilee. You've probably read the story. Jesus was obviously tired because once the boat began to gently sway, He settled in and fell sound asleep. But then, out of the blue, as is common on the Sea of Galilee, a storm whipped up. The disciples, some of whom were professional fishermen, were so frightened they thought they were going to die.

Can you imagine the conversation?

"How can he sleep through this? You need to wake him up."

"You wake him up."

"No, you wake him up."

I don't know how long it went on for, or who eventually shook Jesus awake. When Jesus woke up, He instantly spoke to the wind and waves, silencing the storm and saving the disciples' lives. But I find His reaction fascinating.

Jesus didn't say, "Phew, that was a close one! Thanks for waking me up so I could use my supernatural power to save our lives." No.

The first words out of Jesus' mouth were this: "You of little faith." Jesus rebuked the disciples for not having faith. There they were, staring imminent death in the face, and Jesus scolded them for their lack of faith.

Do you really think the Son of Man was going to die in a drowning accident because He was asleep? With Jesus in the boat, nothing was going to happen. The disciples were left amazed, "Even the wind and waves obey him!"[28]

Even with the big things in life, the situations that rock our world to the core, Jesus can be trusted. We need to turn our focus away from the waves, and onto our Saviour. He calls us to a life of faith over fear.

***

Like an athlete who grows stronger with training, our faith grows stronger when we practise. We can learn to trust God with little things, and as we experience His faithfulness, we begin to trust God with big things too. When we see God at work, when He comes through in a situation we were concerned about, our faith is stronger next time. And, eventually, when things happen that are out of our control, rather than our first reaction being worry and fear, we look to God and experience His peace.

Last year another abnormality was detected in my routine mammogram screen. I had to go back for further tests, including a needle biopsy. What they found wasn't a cyst; it was more serious. But I didn't get caught in the worry spiral this time. I felt a lot more peace in the waiting and was able to carry on enjoying my week while I waited for the results to come through.

When I had my first scare, I was already overwhelmed with the stress of life. I was busy, studying and working and running my household. I was already stretched to the limit and had no capacity to process a serious diagnosis.

The second time, when the finding was potentially more serious, I was less worried. Perhaps it was because I had been through the process before and knew the futility of worrying. But perhaps, it was because I was in a mentally and emotionally healthier place. I had capacity. I had a positive mindset. I felt strong enough to deal with whatever was going to happen.

Next time you feel overwhelmed with worry or anxious thoughts, try praying through Philippians 4:6.

Do not be anxious about anything, but in every

situation, by prayer and petition, with thanksgiving, present your requests to God.

Whenever you are feeling anxious, turn your worries into prayers. Thank God for the good things you have and ask Him for what you need. Then, you will reap the rewards of the next verse.

And the peace of God, which transcends all understanding, will guard your hearts and your minds in Christ Jesus.[29]

What a wonderful promise! Can you imagine the peace of God standing guard around your heart and mind, protecting it from anxiety? This is the truth of what God wants for us.

God doesn't want us to be crippled by the burden of our worries. He wants us to be free, to trust in Him, the one who stills storms, and to enjoy the peace and joy that is beyond our circumstances.

TAKE TIME TO REFLECT

☼ Do you struggle with a cycle of worrying thoughts?
☼ Does your racing mind keep you awake at night?
☼ Do you find it hard to trust God when life is uncertain and circumstances are difficult?
☼ Does the soundtrack in your mind fill you with anxiety?

Here are some practical steps to lay this burden down:

- Write a list of the things you are concerned about and pray through Philippians 4:6, turning your worries into prayers, and asking God for help.

- Practise gratitude. Every morning, list at least three things you are grateful for and give thanks to God.

- Try memorising Scripture to fill your mind with words of truth and faith. Write the words of a favourite Bible verse on a Post-it note in a prominent place and repeat it throughout the day until you know it by heart.

- Notice what you are thinking about and practise taking captive every thought.

6

AM I NOT PRETTY ENOUGH?

THE BURDEN OF PHYSICAL APPEARANCE

My first serious boyfriend, bless his heart, offered to pay half for me to get cosmetic surgery to get my ears fixed. Yep. My ears stick out. I was teased with names like Mickey Mouse and Taxi Doors when I was in primary school. I knew my ears were prominent, but the idea of surgery seemed extreme. I laughed off his offer.

But something stuck.

I loved flipping through Dolly magazine as a teen. It

was the closest thing we had to social media back in the eighties. I remember reading one article in particular. It was a checklist of qualities you need to be a model. It seemed that modelling was the ultimate career goal of all teenage girls in the eighties. I remember reading through the list with my family around the kitchen table—height, weight, bust size, hair length, complexion—we went through the whole list, and I didn't meet any of the criteria. Not one. We had a good laugh as a family. There it was in black and white—I can never be a model. And I didn't really want to be.

But something stuck.

I went shopping with my mother-in-law for my birthday one year. I commented on the uncomfortably low neckline of a top I was trying on. "Don't worry," she said, "you've got nothing to see anyway." I laughed it off.

But the memory of that comment stuck.

And that's how it goes. Like Post-it notes, little comments stick.

Mickey Mouse, taxi doors, shrimp (did I mention how short I am?). The names stick.

All these little comments are very sticky. They stayed on me as I got older, and new sticky comments layered on top. These became the labels that defined my identity—ears too big, legs too short, breasts too small... the list goes on.

And while the comments of others stick, no one makes a crueller assessment of my body than I do. The voice in my head is the most critical of all. Boy, can I explain in excruciating detail the faults of my body. It has many faults. And I have spent way too much time contemplating them.

***

We are constantly given messages that we are not good enough, and after a while, if we're not careful, we start believing them. You will be more beautiful if you use this cream. Your hair will be shiny and lustrous if you buy this treatment. You need these jeans to make you look skinny, and these shoes to make you look tall, and this makeup to help you look young because looking skinny, tall and young will make you happy, successful and popular.

I love the Caroline Caldwell quote, "In a society that profits from your self-doubt, liking yourself is a rebellious act."[30] Rebellion doesn't come naturally to most of us. Our constant self-loathing keeps us self-absorbed and susceptible to every self-improvement movement anyone dreams up for their own profit.

I was very fortunate to grow up in the eighties before the internet and social media were invented. I feel for the youth of today who have so much body comparison to deal with. My exposure to media was limited. I had to save up to buy magazines. We only had three television channels to watch on one TV set that was shared by our family of seven. I wasn't constantly bombarded with the body-shaming messages we get today. Now, it never lets up. It is relentless.

The whole beauty industry seemed much more contained then. I don't remember any big makeup stores in our shopping malls back then. Now they are everywhere, screaming at us all to improve the way we look. Even when they say the message is one of body positivity, they are in the business of making money out of our body discontent. Their job is to convince us all that we need improvement, and that we should spend our money on their product to feel better about ourselves. Their profits depend on us wanting to look younger, skinnier and firmer. If we all loved our natural bodies, they would go out of business.

I find it helpful just reminding myself that I am being fed marketing messages, which is different to being told the truth by someone who loves me. Each message needs to be put in its rightful place. Sales talk is convincing me I need to buy something. They will tell me whatever will make me want to buy, whether it is true or not. They don't care about me. They don't know me. They don't care about my fine lines and wrinkles. They only want to make money by convincing me that there is something wrong with my face.

There is a generation who are growing up constantly bombarded with images of beauty that are manufactured to convince them of their flaws. And it breaks my heart. Don't believe them, ladies. They are lying to you. And it's destroying lives.

***

One of my favourite things to do is to sit on the edge of a cafe in the middle of the city mall and watch people walk by. There is such a diverse variety of people in the city at lunchtime. Every age and stage of life is represented, every body shape and size, every colour of skin tone and style of hairdo. And every wild and wonderful display of self-expression. I love seeing how people express their personal style. I notice well-put-together outfits and get ideas to copy. And I especially love how often I see people confidently wearing combinations I would never wear in a million years.

Spots with stripes, no problem. Tailored suit with sneakers? Sure can. A frilly cocktail dress with chunky boots? Watch me stride! Whatever it is, just wear it.

Sitting in the cafe, sipping my iced long black, makes me realise there is no right or wrong when it comes to style. You can wear whatever you want.

I look at the bodies and faces of people walking by and I wonder what they think about themselves. Do they look in the mirror and only see flaws? Do they feel as strong as they look? Do they realise how beautiful they are? Do they appreciate just how complex and intricate and amazing they are?

I can get caught up with Pinterest advice on how to perfectly style an outfit with the right proportions for my body type, how to tuck my shirt in the right way, how to choose the correct shoes and how to avoid the dreaded visible panty line. But watching real people out in the real world proves it—nobody cares half as much as I do, and I can break all the 'rules' and still look amazing.

Because my body is marvellous. God made it, He knew what He was doing, and He did a great job.

**

My absolute nightmare is shopping for swimwear. For someone who doesn't like their body, all that skin in a full-length all-angle mirror is the height of intimidation. I would prefer to do almost anything else. Trying on different styles of togs seems to highlight every lump, bump and imperfection I hate about my body. The whole process makes me feel self-conscious, embarrassed and horrible about myself. I would end up with a suit that covers as much of my body as possible.

Then, Murray and I started hiking in national parks. We travelled to beautiful parts of the country and went on long hikes, often on hot days. And at the end of many of these hikes were beautiful waterfalls and swimming holes. Avoiding a soak in the cool, clear water was not an option, and wearing a full one-piece swimsuit was hot and impractical for a day of hiking. Eventually, I plucked up the courage to try a bikini.

And this moment changed my life.

I ventured out of the bedroom, wearing my new bikini to show my husband. He looked at my body. And he didn't say, "Have you considered surgery for your ears?" He didn't say, "You will never be a model." And he didn't say my breasts were too small or my belly too big or my legs too short. No.

My husband looked at me, and with tears in his eyes, whispered, "You are so beautiful."

He saw me at my most vulnerable and lifted me up. He saw me and loved me.

I have wet tissues all over the desk as I write about this memory. I don't know if Murray even remembers this day or what he said to me. It might shock him to learn the impact it had on me when he reads this chapter. It was such a powerful moment for me. God gave me an indescribable blessing when He gave me my husband.

I think differently when I feel beautiful rather than feeling self-conscious. I walk differently. I engage with the world differently. There is a freedom that is hard to explain.

And this is what God thinks about me. But I didn't believe God until my godly husband showed me what love for my body looked like.

Bit by bit, I developed the confidence to stop thinking about myself, stop thinking that everyone I saw was judging my body, and fully immerse myself in the beauty of my surroundings. I swam in oceans and lakes all around the country. I felt the sting of waterfall spray on my face, the quiet of floating down remote gorges, and the tickle of tiny fish tasting my legs. One day an enormous manta ray came to say hello in the shallows of the reef. I snorkelled in an untouched coral reef and was engulfed by a massive bait ball. I had exhilarating encounters with nature when I stopped fixating on my body and decided to experience life to the fullest in the body God gave me.

My wish for every single one of you reading this book is to have someone in your life who looks at you and reminds you just how beautiful you are, the more often the better. Because this is the truth of who you are. This is who God created you to be—beautiful.

***

While we were travelling, I spent three years without wearing makeup or blow-drying my hair. There was no point. We were out in the bush where there was no one to impress or fit in with. We spent time in tiny towns where no one else seemed to wear makeup. They were hardworking farmers and country women who had much more important things to do than preen over their eyebrows.

It took me a while to get used to it. At first, I was not used to seeing my natural face and un-styled hair every day. But I did get used to it and learned to love my face again. I swapped my makeup and blow dryer for a big hat and sunscreen and got outside to experience the wonder of creation without putting my appearance at the centre of my attention. It was freeing. I will never forget it. I miss it. I am now back living in the city, and once again I put makeup on and style my hair most days. But I have a different perspective now. I see it for what it is—false, unimportant, low priority, optional, entirely my choice.

Body image issues are a heavy weight to carry. A weight Jesus wants us to lay down. It is not helpful or God-honouring to be constantly concerned about our appearance. God made our bodies. How insulting for us to be so dissatisfied with His handiwork.

That is what we are—God's handiwork. Our bodies have

God's fingerprints all over them. Read that sentence again, slowly. We are each carefully sculpted, unique and individual. Each of us resembles our Creator in our own special way. We resemble Him. We reflect Him. And the way we honour our body is an act of worship to Him.

The Psalmist expressed it like this:

> *For you created my inmost being; you knit me together in my mother's womb. I praise you because I am fearfully and wonderfully made; your works are wonderful, I know that full well.*[31]

I often associate this verse with the wonder of a newborn baby. And that is appropriate. There is nothing more amazing than the grip of a tiny fist around your finger. But that's not what the Psalmist is writing about. He is praising God for his own body. David is looking at himself and saying, "Wow, God, you outdid yourself this time. I am one amazing human! You did a great job when you put my body together."

You're beautiful, just the way you are. Don't believe the lie that you are somehow a better person if you are skinny and young, have clear skin and long, shiny hair. Your appearance does not have any bearing on your value as a person or how much you're loved as a child of God. They are not connected. Being beautiful according to some arbitrary standards invented by a cosmetic company or fashion house does not affect your value as a woman.

You are so much more than your body. I know you know this is true—we all do. But we live in a culture where women are exploited, criticised, and judged for their bodies. Things are slowly changing. There are more plus-sized and mature-age models now on the runways and in advertising. Sexism is being called out and exploitation is no longer acceptable. But somehow the stench of it lives in our cultural subconscious.

Being obsessed with our appearance can be like a cage that limits every other aspect of our lives. Body image is a hard taskmaster that limits our freedom and joy. We can only ever go as far as our cage will allow.

Our actual body seems to have little impact on our body image issues. I've known stunningly beautiful young women who hate their bodies. They battle low self-confidence and insecurity. It ruins their health, their relationships, their budgets, and professional lives. And it can make being friends with them really hard work. Insecure friends who need constant reassurance and encouragement can drain the fun out of every adventure.

And I also know women who have very normal bodies, women like me who will never grace the cover of a beauty magazine, who are strong, confident, smart, and successful. In fact, one of the smartest academics I know, a leader in her field of theology, has a body disfigured by muscular dystrophy and uses a motorised wheelchair to get around. The university where she now lectures had to install a lift when she joined the faculty because the lecture rooms were not accessible. She does not allow her body to hold her back from her calling and passion.

There is so much more to life when we lay down the idol of our appearance. Our body is a simple tool that enables us to serve God and serve others.

The Apostle Paul reminds us to "Offer your bodies as a living sacrifice, holy and pleasing to God—this is your true and proper worship."[32] He goes on to say a few verses later, "Do not think of yourself more highly than you ought, but rather think of yourself with sober judgment".[33]

Lay your body down on the altar of God. Give your body back to Him, and experience life to the full, fully free and fully loved. Don't obsess over your appearance. Take your focus off yourself and focus on what is truly important.

I spent some time this week with the senior's group at our church. Most of these precious saints are eighty years old or older. They have frail bodies and strong faith. They are a blessing to spend time with because they have their priorities right. They love God and love each other in such an inspirational way, and they are generous with their encouragement.

The group call themselves The Ascenders. They have their eyes on Heaven. Their greatest delight is their relationship with their Saviour, and they are looking forward to looking at His face and kneeling in His presence. These saints live in the reality of Philippians 3:20–21:

> *But our citizenship is in heaven. And we eagerly await a Saviour from there, the Lord Jesus Christ, who, by the power that enables him to bring everything under his control, will transform our lowly bodies so that they will be like his glorious body.*

One day we will have a new body. And somehow, I doubt that "Does my bum look big in this?" will be one of the questions I ask when I get it. Our body is temporary. Let's not waste eternal energy on temporary concerns.

***

I understand there is a tricky balance to navigate; we can't neglect caring for our bodies.

There is a difference between health and beauty. While I do not in any way think that anyone is more or less valuable or worthwhile depending on their body size or shape, the health of our bodies is an important responsibility. God wants us to take care of our bodies. Our body is the temple of the Holy Spirit, it is a living sacrifice, it is a gift from our Creator to be cherished and cared for. And we only get one. We have one body that has to last our whole lives. And when we don't take care of it, life gets very difficult.

I know there are a lot of health challenges that we have no control over. Healthy people still get struck with unexplained illnesses that can be serious and even fatal. But there is a lot we can do to prevent illness and prolong our lives. Maintaining a healthy weight, eating fresh food, getting enough sleep and regular exercise all contribute to a healthy body. They are hard work. But taking care of our bodies is an act of worship.

We need to be healthy to do God's work. We were created for a purpose.

For we are God's handiwork, created in Christ Jesus to do good works, which God prepared in advance for us to do.[34]

We need a body to do those good works. We need a body to enjoy God's creation. We need a body to love and care for our family and friends, to work and to play. Our body is important.

So, when do we know we've crossed the line between caring for our bodies and being obsessed with our appearance? I can't answer that for you. I think there are a lot of different circumstances and contexts that affect where that line is for each of us. For me, it is when my appearance becomes a burden. When my focus is more on what I look like than on my character, I have a problem. Because character trumps appearance every time.

Think about women you admire. Who would you call in the middle of the night during an emergency? Who do you talk to when you feel lost, overwhelmed or stuck?

Who are the women you admire for their courage, wisdom, insight and encouragement? The women who are kind and helpful, the ones who help you find perspective, hold you accountable, and keep your secrets. Can you see their faces? Can you list their names? The list may include your mother and grandmother, aunts and in-laws. There may be friends and mentors in your church or from your past. They may be other mothers from school or colleagues from work.

Does their physical appearance form part of the criteria? Does their height and weight matter?

What criteria are on the list when you think about what you love about them? When we are seeking advice, a listening ear, a supportive friend, we don't call our most beautiful friend; we call the wise woman of character. In fact, appearance doesn't really make it to the list. The people we love to spend time with, the people we call when we need help and support, are women with godly character, and appearance is completely irrelevant.

Remember this verse from Proverbs 31?

> *Charm is deceptive, and beauty is fleeting; but a woman who fears the Lord is to be praised.*[35]

Ultimately, our character is so much more important than our appearance. Who we are is more important than what we look like.

My dream is to love and appreciate my body enough to look after it really well—eat clean, fresh food, exercise regularly and get plenty of sleep, wear clothes that I feel confident in, and feel healthy and strong. And then, when all of the above is part of my daily routine, I don't want to think about my body anymore. I don't want to be stressing over wrinkles or silver hair or whether I have the right shoes for my outfit. I don't want to wear special underwear that sucks me in and smooths me out. I don't want to feel self-conscious or embarrassed about my ears, my breasts or my height. I don't ever want to be distracted by thinking about what other people are thinking about my clothes or my hair or my face. I want to be me—healthy, happy, confident me. Absolutely beautiful, totally free, completely loved. The me God created me to be.

And that is my dream for you too.

TAKE TIME TO REFLECT

☼ What is your relationship with your body like? Do you feel self-conscious or confident?

☼ Are you always buying the latest anti-aging lotions and potions? Do you find yourself on an endless cycle of dieting?

☼ Does your attitude toward your body limit the activities you're involved in because you feel embarrassed or concerned about what others will think of you?

Here are some practical steps to lay this burden down:

- Thank God for your body. Acknowledge that you are fearfully and wonderfully made in the image of your Creator.

- Go a day without doing your hair or makeup.

- Buy clothes that fit your body rather than trying to fit your body into clothes.

- Tell your daughters, mothers, grandmothers and friends how beautiful they are, often. And not just when they are dressed up for a special occasion.

7

MISTAKES, REGRETS & EMBARRASSING MOMENTS

THE BURDEN OF STRIVING FOR GOD'S LOVE

It was Easter Sunday morning. Murray and I were living in our caravan, on our trip around Australia. We had been on the road for just a few months, learning how to live differently, slowing down to enjoy the beauty of creation. We were in a beautiful national park called Carnarvon Gorge. It is one of the most spectacular places I have ever been in my life.

But we weren't supposed to be there then. We had booked the campsite for a few days to do the walks into the gorge, but when we got there, the walks were closed. There had been a massive weather event a few days prior to our arrival, and the paths were washed out and littered with debris from the storms. The rangers were working to clear and secure the paths, but it would take a few days.

We had a choice. We could leave and plan to return at another time. Many of the campers around us made that choice and headed out to find a better location for their precious vacation days. Or we could extend our stay and wait for the walking tracks to open. This is what we did. Our four-day stay turned into nine. And it was worth the wait. Each walk took us to breathtaking scenery.

But because of our delay, we found ourselves in the bush on Easter Sunday. We were in a campground in the middle of nowhere. The closest town was hours away. There was no church to attend. And the path we had been waiting to trek was open.

So, here I was, on Easter Sunday morning, walking through one of the most majestic gorges in the world. And the overwhelming feeling was guilt. Yep. I just felt guilty. I should have been in church. I should have been celebrating the resurrection with a congregation of believers, not bushwalking.

It felt wrong.

And this is when God broke through. In my mind, I could hear the song, The Blessing. The lyrics echo Numbers 6:24–26, "The Lord bless you and keep you; the Lord make His face shine on you and be gracious to you." It was so clear in my head it was almost audible. "The Lord turn His face toward you and give you peace." It wasn't my voice singing. I couldn't remember the last time I'd sung the song or thought about its lyrics from Numbers. No, it wasn't me. "May His favour be upon you, And a thousand generations."[36] I became aware of my God singing a blessing over me. The God of Heaven and Earth, Creator of the universe, was smiling down on me.

I heard God say to me, "Look around at this beautiful cathedral I have created for you to worship me. This is what I want from you today—enjoy Me." Something shifted in me that Sunday morning.

God lifted the burden of guilt from my heart and reminded me of His unconditional love.

I find it so easy to imagine God's disapproval when I examine my life. I can replay in excruciating detail the mistakes I have made, like a movie in my mind. And the feeling of my shame in those moments comes alive again. I can hear my heart pounding loud in my ears, my breath shallow and quick, the butterflies in my stomach, as if I was being caught red-handed all over again. And I'm particularly good at replaying all my most awful moments when I am tired and stressed.

I can remember when my father caught me stealing change from his drawer to buy ice cream at the school canteen. As a beginning classroom teacher, I remember being berated by a more experienced teacher for not managing the behaviour of my class correctly. I still want the stage to swallow me up when I recall getting lost in a song when I was leading worship one Sunday morning. I remember the song. I remember what I did wrong. I remember having a quiet cry when I was finally alone. I can relive these moments, and many, many more. Like a jukebox, I can push the button, and the track begins to play.

I can remember so many difficult and emotionally charged conversations over my years in ministry. I remember being misunderstood and misrepresented. I remember being blamed for other people's decisions. I bore the brunt of people's hurt and frustration. All the memories are right there, on speed dial, ready to replay. And I used to lie awake at night and repeat those difficult conversations word for word, years later.

But whether those instances were because of the mistakes I made or the consequences of others around me, the weight of the burden, the replay of my shame, is not something that comes from God. Because God's love is not something that we earn by avoiding mistakes or doing everything right.

***

It makes sense for love to follow a brownie point system. It's natural. We all keep a secret tally in our hearts. "If you love me, I will love you." Or, "If you hurt me, I will withdraw my love until you deserve it back." We often don't acknowledge or articulate it; our tally is kept deep inside. It may never be written down or spoken about, but you always know if you are in brownie point surplus or deficit.

We unwittingly apply this tally system to our relationship with God. Somewhere deep inside, we unconsciously think God will love us more if we are good. When we do the right thing, read our Bible, pray, and go to church every single week (especially with the kids in tow), we feel like we deserve God's love. We accept it and enjoy it. We work hard to keep the brownie point tally in the positive and earn the love we deserve.

And when we fail, when we lie or steal or cheat, when we get angry, selfish or lazy, we feel guilty and undeserving of God's love. In this brownie point deficit, we withdraw from God and often from Christian community as well. We feel unworthy, and it makes us ashamed to show our face before God.

Adam and Eve experienced this. When they disobeyed God and sinned, they withdrew, hiding in the garden rather than walking in God's presence. They tried to cover their nakedness, suddenly aware and ashamed of themselves. And this story is repeated over and over in history and our own lives. It is our nature.

When we've done wrong, we feel like God wouldn't want anything to do with us. We expect Him to reject us. But He doesn't reject us. Rather, He invites us into His very throne room to ask Him for everything we need, with the confidence of a child running towards a generous and loving father.

> *Let us then approach God's throne of grace with confidence, so that we may receive mercy and find grace to help us in our time of need.*[37]

We don't have to run away and hide. We can run towards God and confidently ask Him for everything we need. Brownie points to spare or not.

When we understand the reality of God's grace, it changes everything. When we get it, that God's love is not conditional on our behaviour, the posture of our heart is completely different. We stop keeping a tally of brownie points. The weight of being 'good enough' is lifted. God isn't keeping a scorecard or tally of the good and bad you do and punishing you if you get out of balance. No, God's love is unconditional. How He feels about us doesn't change depending on how we behave.

Unconditional. Think about that. God's love has no conditions. You can't earn it, you don't deserve it, you can't change it. It's unconditional. It's so unfair!

We can't make God love us more. It doesn't matter how good we are. No matter how much we work for Him, sacrifice for Him, give to the church or serve the poor, we can't get any more of His love. We expect love to be transactional. We presume God will bless us more if we do things for Him, but it doesn't work that way.

My husband has always been a very generous man. He has the spiritual gift of giving, no doubt. As a small business owner, there have been times of plenty, and we have been able to generously bless our church, several missionaries and even personal friends who were in difficult circumstances from time to time. This was always done cheerfully without any expectation of anything in return. Until. Murray's business failed, and he had a long period of looking for work, firstly projects for his business and eventually, when all channels were exhausted, looking for employment. During this period, there were several people who took advantage of Murray, breaking promises, not honouring contracts, and trying to steal intellectual property. It was a very difficult time.

A number of times during these years, Murray asked for prayer, standing bravely and allowing others to come alongside him and pray. It was difficult, even humiliating, that someone with a successful work life spanning thirty years stood with the unemployed, seeking divine intervention. But that wasn't the most difficult part. You see, God didn't answer that prayer. It didn't work, and the transactional mindset was impossible to shake. We were generous to God, and He didn't honour that. God didn't send the work that we needed. He didn't prevent dishonest people from ripping us off. God wasn't generous back to us, and it felt so unfair. Eventually, we had to sell our house.

You read that right. We sold our house. It was one of the saddest days of our lives. When the hammer fell, and the auctioneer yelled, "Sold!" with excitement, congratulating the winning bidder, we hit a low we never imagined. It felt like God had abandoned us. But, as it is so often with God, the lowest point in our story was not the end. God had more in store.

God's economy isn't the same as ours. He doesn't count our brownie points and bless us according to how good we are. We see godly people get cancer and die young. It's not fair. We see hard-working businessmen and women who operate with integrity lose everything they have, and families who are devoted to following Jesus battle chronic illness, disability, and personal injury.

God's unconditional love isn't fair.

It works the other way as well. There is nothing we can do to make God love us any less. It doesn't matter how bad we are. God won't stop loving us. This is also unfair. When we least deserve it, God loves us. When we were still sinners, Christ died for us. We can make mistakes, we can fail and give in to temptation and mess up our lives, and God forgives us. He removes our sin from us as far as the East is from the West. He remembers them no more! What a wonderful gift. We may struggle to forgive ourselves, and the devil loves to remind us of our mistakes so we can waste precious sleep hours replaying our disgrace in our minds, but God forgives and forgets.

We can find it hard to imagine God loving people who do truly evil things. We expect there is a limit to the negative brownie point scale. But no. God loves murderers, abusers, adulterers, and drug dealers. God loves the vilest offenders who we feel don't deserve to breathe. He loves them just as much as He loves you and me. The same amount.

Jesus demonstrated this in a profound way when He was on the cross. Jesus was crucified between two criminals who deserved to die. One of them had no time for Jesus. The other one, however, cried out to Jesus in his final moments and asked for His help. Jesus, knowing that this thief would not do one good work, would not give one cent to charity, would not contribute to the Kingdom in any way whatsoever, granted his cry for salvation and gave him the gift of eternal life. Jesus saved a man who lived a godless life; a criminal whose crimes deserved the punishment of death.

I am not saying that sin doesn't have consequences. It does. Bad ones. When we reject God and live outside of His truth, we can make a serious mess of our lives and cause ourselves and the people we love enormous pain. Some sins may be fun and exciting for a period of time, but they fail to satisfy the longings in our hearts, and they always eventually lead to death. But ruining our lives does not change the way God feels about us; He loves us just the same.

We want love to be fair. It should be equal on both sides of the equation. When someone loves us and expresses that love in acts of service and kindness, we expect to reciprocate. We give back. We live in a way that is deserving of that love.

When it comes to God's love, we are overwhelmingly in debt. We can't do anything to deserve the love God lavishes on us. As hard as we try, as much as we work, we can never add up to enough. We can strive and strive and strive and will always come up short. We have a choice. We can either accept the gift of God's love or continue to feel the weight of the debt and keep working to pay our way.

***

The one place the brownie point system never worked for me was with my children. The moment I held each of my children for the first time, my heart was full of brownie points that have never diminished. Becoming a mother helped me understand what unconditional love felt like from the lover's perspective.

My babies did nothing to deserve my love. They didn't earn my love. The love I felt for them was not connected to how intelligent, attractive or productive they were. It was years before any of my children did anything helpful. The only thing they brought into my life was hard work and self-sacrifice. Yet, despite this, my heart was full to overflowing with love for them before I had even seen their faces.

As they grew, I taught them to be helpful. I encouraged them to show their love in acts of kindness and generosity. I expected them to contribute to the running of the household. But my love never changed dependent on the contribution they made. They didn't receive less love during times of busyness or sickness when they needed more care. They didn't receive more of my love when they did the dishes more often. It just doesn't work that way.

Living with this knowledge helped me to better understand God's love for me. It is good for us to contribute to His Kingdom: to give generously, carry one another's burdens and help those in need. But God's love for us doesn't depend on our ability to work. Those who are elderly, unwell or disabled do not receive any less of God's love than those who give their lives in service to the Kingdom. Just like my children.

And this unconditional love spills out into generosity.

I love giving gifts to my kids. Now they are older, I love paying the bill when we go out to eat. I love finding the perfect gift. When they were young, I remember spending hours researching and shopping for toys that would light up their faces on Christmas morning. I loved buying them clothes that made them feel confident and shoes with glittery heels or whatever it was that lit up their smile and gave them the assurance to step out into the big wide world.

Murray and I were reminiscing recently while we sat in a park having a cup of coffee by a playground. We fondly remember the Christmas Eve Murray's dad came around to our place at 8:30 pm, after the children were asleep, to put together a new swing set. Father and Grandfather worked long into the night building the swings in our backyard. It was hard work. It was also a delight to hear the excited squeals of our children the next morning, eyes wide, as they ran into the yard. Those swings brought many hours of joy, and we all remembered how they magically appeared on Christmas morning.

I love giving generous gifts to my kids. But sometimes, I don't recognise how much God loves to give generous gifts to me. I expect that God will be frugal and stingy, carefully counting out the scraps of blessing so as not to spend too much on me or give me more than I deserve. And this is what led to Easter Sunday in Carnarvon Gorge, focused inward, feeling guilty for not being in church rather than delighting in my generous, Creator God and the incredible gift He wanted to give me that morning.

God is not stingy with His gifts to us. No, He loves to see the faces of His children light up in delight.

> *See what great love the Father has lavished on us, that we should be called children of God! And that is what we are!*[38]

God is extravagant with His gifts for His children. He loves the delight in my eyes when I accept and acknowledge gifts from Him.

> *If you, then, though you are evil, know how to give good gifts to your children, how much more will your Father in heaven give good gifts to those who ask him!*[39]

Don't glance over the truth of these verses. Read them again. We are children of God. And our Heavenly Father loves to give us gifts when we ask Him. We don't have to hide when we feel our most vulnerable. We can reach out to Him instead. God paid the ultimate price, the life of His Son, Jesus, so He could have a relationship with you and me. Yes, God gave up His one and only Son to have a relationship with us. His sacrifice is the ultimate example of love.

We don't need to carry the weight of our sin. He took it, so we don't have to.

There is no brownie point tally. There is no scale with good on one side and bad on the other. There is no point in striving for God's love. It is already absolute. We are loved. We are free.

So in the quiet moments, when I'm tired and I've had a bad day and the movie of my past mistakes begins to play, I simply remind myself, "God is not thinking about this. Why are you?" When God looks at me, He doesn't shake His head; He smiles. So why do I shake my head at myself?

The devil loves to remind us of our past mistakes because it cripples us. It keeps us small and contained. Or, we keep pulling out the victim hat, reliving all the bad things that others have done to us over the years. We examine our scars and massage our bruises, and we miss all the blessings that God wants to lavish on us today.

I'm not trying to diminish the pain that I know some of you have suffered. There is deep trauma that we carry because of the injustice of life in this sin-drenched world that so many have to endure. But God made a way for us to lay our shame and guilt down and accept His unconditional love and extravagant gifts. We don't have to strive to deserve God's love. This is not a burden God gives us to carry.

TAKE TIME TO REFLECT

- ☼ Do you feel weighed down by feelings of guilt and shame? Do you feel like you need to behave a certain way to earn God's love? Do you withdraw from God and others when you make mistakes, feeling unworthy?

- ☼ Do the memories of past mistakes hold you back from experiencing joy in the present?

- ☼ Do you struggle to love others when they are not behaving in a loving way toward you?

Here are some practical steps to lay this burden down:

- Confess your sins and ask for forgiveness. First John 1:9 says, "If we confess our sins, he is faithful and just and will forgive us our sins and purify us from all unrighteousness."

- Ask God to help you forgive others who have hurt you and forgive yourself for the mistakes you have made. When thoughts of shame haunt you, remind yourself that you are forgiven.

- Accept God's extravagant love. Do something you love and imagine God smiling down on you. Buy yourself flowers, eat your favourite ice cream, or do some other activity that fills you with joy.

8

BIGGER IS BETTER

THE BURDEN OF OUR POSSESSIONS

"Sold!" the auctioneer yelled excitedly. There had been spirited bidding from three couples to buy our beautiful home. Then came the enthusiastic handshakes, smiles and relief in the family room.

But for me and Murray, the opposite emotion filled our hearts. Our home was gone. We no longer owned a house. We felt empty. We felt like failures. We felt shame. We smiled reassuringly at our children.

And we grieved for all we had worked for and lost.

It was September 2017. Our two girls were in university, and our son was in his senior year of high school. It was our family's rock bottom. God hadn't answered our prayers for Murray's work the way we wanted, even after looking for any other solution to our financial situation.

The next weeks were a blur. We had to find a suitable rental home to move into and get rid of a lot of stuff: furniture, decor, musical instruments that no longer got played, sporting equipment that had sat in the garage since our children were small—so much stuff! Boxes and boxes of it.

We had bought into the great Australian dream and borrowed the maximum amount allowed to buy the biggest house in the nicest neighbourhood we could. We had two nice cars in the garage. Then, as our kids grew, two cars became five—one for each of us, and all a different colour. This is what successful families do. We were normal.

We had a big, beautiful home. It had three spacious living areas, four big bedrooms and separate office spaces for Murray and me. It was very comfortable to live in.

When we bought the home, we could easily afford the repayments. Murray's business was going well, and I was working three days a week at church. But slowly, over time, things changed. The computer industry began to change, and the demand for custom software dwindled. After a year of R&D work, a contract fell through, and the next one was difficult to pull over the line. The work dried up, and my part-time income didn't come close to covering our expenses.

How big of a hole do you dig before you give up?

We made a heartbreaking decision and put our home up for sale.

We decided to take advantage of an enthusiastic housing

market in our area and get out of debt. Then, we could take a breath and explore options for what was next. But, boy, it felt horrible at the time. The process of staging, selling, and moving was hard—really hard.

That big house represented so many things we valued. It was a symbol of success. It was our security; the place we called home. It was a place of comfort and safety, a place where our kids could bring their friends after school for milkshakes or after church for tacos. It was a home full of laughter and fun, arguments and slammed doors (teenagers!). It was within walking distance from school. It was within walking distance of their first jobs and their first loves. It was our family home.

It was also full of stuff we didn't need and space we didn't use. But we didn't recognise that at the time. That came later.

We found a house to rent that was about two-thirds the size of the house we sold. It still had four bedrooms and two living areas, an office for Murray to work in, space for our big family dining table, and room for our hand-me-down piano.

We got rid of everything that didn't fit, gave furniture away to friends and family, and made multiple trips to the donation centre and rubbish dump. In the end, a second-hand furniture dealer came with a truck and a chequebook and took the remainder away. The cheque he wrote wasn't generous, but the garage was clear, and we could begin our new downsized lives—our new debt-free lives.

And an amazing and unexpected thing happened.

We loved it. We didn't tolerate it. We loved it.

We didn't recognise the weight of being in debt until it was gone, and we could breathe again. We didn't miss the extra rooms and the extra stuff. And the important things—the things we loved the most about our home, were still there.

There was still laughter and fun, there were still teenagers arguing and slamming doors. There were still cars of every colour parked in the driveway and friends eating tacos around our dining room table. It was still home.

And with money in the bank and expenses reduced, we were able to make plans for our future.

The weight was gone. The pressure was gone.

We felt free.

All the worry and stress of trying to keep up with the payments was gone. The time I spent cleaning and organising all the stuff in all the rooms was mine again.

Murray invested in training and, a few months later, landed a great new job. Our children grew up, got jobs, got married, and went to start their own lives. Within two years, there were just three of us, and we downsized once again— this time to an apartment in the city. And again, we loved it.

We were sold the lie that a bigger house with a bigger mortgage would make us happy. But it isn't true. Debt is a modern-day form of slavery. It traps us and limits our options. Debt loads on stress, and banks and credit companies are coming up with more and more ways to trap us.

I couldn't have orchestrated this: As I sit at my kitchen table and write, I just received a text message from my bank offering me a $200 bonus if I set up a credit card today. I received an email about the deal a couple of days ago, but the offer is about to expire, so the messages have become more urgent. It is so easy to get tricked into thinking that another credit card would be a good idea, but I now know it isn't. I am being lured into a trap, and I'm not biting.

***

The appeal of money and possessions is not a new one. In fact, Jesus had more to say about money than almost any other topic He taught about. There was one particular encounter with Jesus that always made me uncomfortable.

One day, Jesus was interrupted by a young man looking for answers.

"What must I do to have eternal life?" he asked.

This young man was a student of the Scriptures. He kept the Law. He did all the right things. But he knew something was missing.

Jesus provided an answer to what he was seeking:

> *Go, sell everything you have and give to the poor, and you will have treasure in heaven. Then come, follow me.*[40]

The young man went away sad. The price was too high. He couldn't do what Jesus asked because, the verse before tells us, "He had great wealth."

I feel sorry for this young man. I don't blame him one bit for walking away. I wouldn't have done it either. How does Jesus expect him to live if he gives up all his money? What about the generations before who had worked hard to accumulate the wealth he inherited? What about his children and grandchildren? Don't they deserve to live a financially secure life? Jesus, this is an unreasonable request.

But what if Jesus wasn't trying to ruin this young man's life? What if Jesus knew that all the wealth he owned was actually owning him and that he would be better off without it? What if money makes us miserable, and following Jesus makes us happy? I find this an interesting question to ponder, especially when I read the text message from my bank, literally wanting to pay me to get a credit card.

The beginning of the verse I quoted above reads, "Jesus

looked at him and loved him." Jesus loved this young man who was trying so hard to do everything right. Jesus loved him and wanted the very best for him, in this life and in eternity. Jesus wasn't trying to make this young man's life harder. Jesus wasn't cursing him, testing him, or sentencing him to a life of poverty and struggle. So, what did Jesus know that we don't?

Perhaps Jesus knew the weight of this man's wealth was weighing down his heart and mind. Perhaps he was overwhelmed with worry. Perhaps he spent all his time managing, sorting, counting, cleaning, insuring and protecting his money and the things he had purchased. Perhaps managing his business interests and keeping on top of his financial obligations was enslaving him, and Jesus wanted him to be free.

This is my experience. But I would never have given up our big house voluntarily. If Jesus had asked me beforehand, I would have said no, just like the rich young ruler.

But God, in His kindness, didn't ask for my permission. He took it away, gently prising my fingers from the false security I was clinging to so hard. And He gave us something far greater in return. Freedom. Peace of mind. Joy. Contentment.

I honestly can't describe the feeling; once the house was sold, the excess was cleared, and we settled in our smaller home—it was like someone lifted a pile of bricks from our chests and we took a deep breath for the first time in months, or maybe even years.

A deep, slow breath, followed by another, and another. Ahh.

And we began to learn that our security was not in our home or our possessions. My identity is not in my wardrobe or shoes. Hospitality did not depend on my impressive home. It was always in God.

What we thought was the biggest failure of our lives ended up being the doorway to our biggest joy. And isn't that so often the way with God? We struggle to give something up, only to be given something so much greater in return. He is so kind.

***

In the parable of the sower, Jesus describes different kinds of soil, depicting the condition of the human heart and its receptiveness to the word of God. One of the soil types is the thorny soil. When Jesus was explaining the meaning of the thorny soil later to the disciples, He explains, the deceitfulness of wealth and the worries of the world crowd out the word, so it is not fruitful.[41]

The deceitfulness of wealth crowds our lives, so we can't be fruitful. We don't have the space we need to grow to our full potential. We are choked out by thorns. But wealth is oh, so deceitful! We get sucked in. The evil one uses the consumeristic culture around us to coax us into owning more than we need. Because he knows it will crowd our lives and take up all the space we would have for a fruitful faith.

I know from experience that the bigger our home, the more time and energy it requires to take care of. We had to clean it, organise all the stuff in it, maintain it, insure it and protect it. It's a lot. And for so many years, this took up more of my life than it needed to. I know what it feels like to be choking in stuff. The average American home holds 300,000 items.[42] I can't imagine the Australian statistics are different. And every one of those 300,000 things requires something of us.

When is enough, enough? How much do we really need?

The apostle Paul wrote one of the most famous faith-building verses in the entire Bible. He says, "I can do all things through him who gives me strength."⁴³ And we all agree, yes and amen. But what is Paul actually talking about in this passage? What is the context of this statement?

Paul is talking about contentment. The preceding verse says:

> *I know what it is to be in need, and I know what it is to have plenty. I have learned the secret of being content in any and every situation, whether well fed or hungry, whether living in plenty or in want.*

And the very next sentence is,

> *I can do all this through him who gives me strength.*⁴⁴

In God's strength we can learn to be content. And we need God's strength to be content, because our culture does not value or celebrate contentment. It celebrates materialism, greed, and excess. It celebrates designer clothes, collections of shoes, square footage and giant screens. It's hard to be content with small and simple. It can be difficult to discern how much is enough.

It takes a lot of confidence in God to lay down the burden of our possessions. Our world values wealth so highly. Having lots of money, or at least the appearance of having lots of money, is the ultimate sign of success. The type of car we drive, the suburb we live in and the brand of clothes we wear changes the way people view us. And our world judges those who are poor, as if there is something wrong with them. So, the idea of intentionally living below our means and appearing to be poorer than we are takes a lot of courage and faith.

But I cannot begin to describe how much better life is now.

As we got rid of more and more of our stuff, I discovered

the beauty of simplicity and a joy in owning less. As the years have gone on, I have embraced a minimalist lifestyle more and more, enjoying owning fewer clothes, only a few pairs of shoes, limited kitchen appliances and only one spare set of towels and sheets. After a lifetime of managing loads of laundry at different stages around the house, shelves of shoes I never wore, a kitchen overflowing with gadgets and a linen cupboard stuffed full of old sheets and towels, having fewer things that are used regularly and enjoyed is a great way to live.

* * *

There were a few simple things I began to do in that season that helped me reorientate my heart to contentment.

Firstly, I stopped going shopping as a leisure activity. There was a time in my life when I used to spend every Friday morning walking the length of my local shopping centre, just for fun. It was my day off work to run errands and clean the house. I was mentally exhausted from a busy week, and I went to the shops to buy the groceries for the week. But rather than just buying food, I would have a coffee and then wander through the shops. And I always came home with a little something. There would be nice towels on sale, or a pretty top would catch my eye. Nothing major. Just little bits and pieces for my family or for my home.

What I didn't realise was that this practice was constantly reinforcing my discontent. Browsing the homewares made me unsatisfied with my towels, sheets, and tea towels. The new-season clothes and shoes were always so much nicer than the old ones in my closet. The advertising around me reminded me again and again that my face was aging, my body was bulging, and my home was dated, reinforcing my discontent every single week.

So I stopped recreational shopping. I still went and purchased the things my family needed, but I no longer mindlessly browsed through shops full of things I didn't need. It took a while, but eventually, knowing I didn't need anything helped me not want anything new.

I also stopped watching the Home Network on TV. I used to love watching all the home flipping, styling, and selling shows and seeing the finished homes, full of colour-coordinated furnishings and carefully styled kitchen islands. My home never looked like that. No one's home actually looks like that, and feeding my mind with these images only reinforced my discontent.

Next, and this sounds counterintuitive, getting rid of two-thirds of my clothes helped me be more content with my wardrobe. Yes, my relationship with clothes improved when I got rid of most of them.

I first donated all my duplicate clothes. Even though I had three black T-shirts, I always reached for the same one. And although I had numerous pairs of black pants, white shirts, and denim jeans, I wore the same ones over and over. The clothes that fit me well, were comfortable to wear, easy to take care of and made me feel confident and attractive were the outfits I reached for.

So, I got rid of everything else. And it was one of the most liberating things I have ever done. I no longer had a wardrobe cluttered with outfits that didn't fit, were uncomfortable or just 'not me'. Getting dressed each morning became easier, my laundry routine became simpler, and I felt more content.

I also stopped grocery shopping. Well, in the traditional sense, anyway. Rather than walking the aisles of the store each week and being manipulated to buy things that were on special or took my fancy, I set up a meal plan and an online grocery order I could pick up on our way home from church each week.

By setting up a few simple structures, I gradually broke the cycle of constantly accumulating more than I needed, and soon, I stopped wanting more than I had. And although I'm not as strict with myself anymore—I go grocery shopping in person again now, and occasionally, I wander through a shopping centre without a list—I am wiser to the manipulation around me and see it for what it is: a trap.

A new pair of shoes that almost fit well won't make a good addition to my wardrobe, even if they are 40% off. And I know the credit card deal is not worth the $200 bonus I'm being offered. I know I don't need more than I have.

I call myself a minimalist, even though you would never walk into my living room and think, "The person who lives here is a minimalist." There are pictures on the wall, cushions on my couch and plants on the shelves. But there are no piles of laundry at various stages. The shelves in my cupboards are not overflowing. There is space to breathe; space to live.

Our ultimate downsize happened four years after we sold our big house. We went from a smaller house, to a large apartment in the city, to a twenty-one-foot caravan to travel around the country. We lived in our RV for almost three years, and I learned how few possessions we really needed, and how much life we had time for without them.

Jesus was right. Our excess possessions weigh us down and crowd our lives.

 **TAKE TIME TO REFLECT**

- ☼ Are you weighed down by excess possessions? Do you have a home full of rooms you don't use and things you don't need?

- ☼ Are you enslaved by debt to pay for your lifestyle?

- ☼ Do you feel discontented with your home, your car, and your clothes? Do you find yourself always wanting more?

Here are some practical steps to lay this burden down:

- Stop shopping. See how long you can go without buying anything new.

- Unsubscribe to promotional emails and texts from stores that tempt you to buy things you don't need.

- Declutter your home. Donate or sell items you no longer use regularly.

- Pray for contentment. Ask God to help you disentangle your heart from the love of money.

9

DO MORE, BE BETTER

THE BURDEN OF LIMITED CAPACITY

You've probably heard the William H. Johnsen quote, "If it is to be, it is up to me." Sounds good, right? Until you try to live by it. Then it feels like the weight of the world is on your shoulders, and it's your responsibility to keep all the balls in the air.

It's up to me.

It's my job to get the kids to school on time, in the correct uniform, with their homework done and a healthy lunch in their bags.

It's up to me.

I need to keep snacks in the pantry, fresh food in the fridge, dinner everyone likes on the table by six and a spare stash of toilet paper in the cupboard.

It's up to me.

Change the sheets, wash the towels, mop the floor, scrub the shower.

It's up to me.

Haircuts, dentist visits, Grandma's birthday, pack for vacation.

It's up to me.

Do you feel tired just reading through this list? Do you carry the mental load of managing your home and family? We keep our families running smoothly. We juggle all the things and remember all the details. We organise all the events and hold the tension of all the relationships. It takes its toll. And that is before we pile on the complexity of a job.

For the first four years of my ministry, I was the programming and production coordinator. It was my job to ensure that Sunday services ran smoothly: there was a worship team rostered on, the right lyrics on the screen, props on stage, handouts at the door and water for the preacher. If the guitar was too loud, the vocalist's skirt too short or there were too many announcements, I had to sort it out.

It's up to me.

Then I changed roles to pastoral care and connection. It was my job to send flowers, help arrange funeral services, sit by hospital beds and pray for the sick and broken hearted. I came face-to-face with grieving families, cancer patients, and people struggling with life and faith challenges. I never knew what situations would come across my path each day. I loved it and found it a real privilege to journey with people through the challenges and joys of life. But even though I loved what I was doing, after a while, I wasn't coping.

I was trying to live by the adage, "It's up to me."

Actually no. It's not. It's not up to me at all. Yet, I felt the weight of it. I struggled under the pressure. And it was more than I could carry. Did I mention that the counselling I received after my panic attack wasn't the first time I needed help? Oh, how I wish I had learned more lessons earlier in my journey.

I had a good friend and colleague who pointed me to a professional counsellor who had experience with people in vocational ministry. My counsellor explained the simple concept of four types of energy: physical, mental, emotional, and spiritual. Each type of energy is distinctive, each is important, and each needs refilling, like a water jar with a tap at the bottom, to pour from the tap it needs to be filled from the top.

My counsellor set me some exercises. I had to record the things I did each day and comment on how they made me feel. How much energy did I have before and after? Did the time fly by, or drag on? Was it a breeze, or a struggle? Was each activity life-giving, or life-draining?

I did a few weeks of intentional energy inventory, and it changed the way I organised my calendar.

I realised that my programming and production job was mostly mentally and physically demanding, and over time I learned how to recognise when I was depleted in these areas and how to refill these energy jars. However, my new pastoral care role was more emotionally and spiritually draining, and I had not yet learned to recognise the warning signs that my energy was running low. I was completely emotionally and spiritually tired and it came out in symptoms of stress, illness, and overwhelm. I wasn't incompetent, just depleted and needing to open the top of the jars and replenish the energy reserves I had been giving out.

By doing the energy inventory, I learned that if I attended a funeral in the morning, whether I had a personal relationship with the deceased or not, I was left emotionally exhausted. Funerals are exhausting. If I got back to my desk after a memorial service and expected to write a sermon or Bible study or make more pastoral care calls, I hit rock bottom. But, if I assigned time to do some of the more mundane physical tasks like printing and collating booklets, or cleaning jobs (that are always waiting to be done), I got to the end of the day and home to my family in a much better place.

Learning about this concept had a huge impact on how I manage my time and my self-care. It all makes perfect sense when you think about it. We all have limited personal capacity. We have a responsibility to manage that capacity carefully to ensure we have what we need in reserve for every area of our lives. There are some things that drain energy out and other things that pour energy in, and there are helpful indicators that reveal when the levels are getting low. If we ignore the warnings, we burn out. Simple as that.

Let's look at each of the four types of energy and some ideas of the kinds of things that empty and fill each jar. There is no one-size-fits-all solution here. We are all wired uniquely and respond to different situations in different ways.

Physical

Physical energy is probably the easiest to understand and manage. We know what it feels like when we're physically tired, and we know what we need to do to refill. We need physical rest. We are not designed to work flat out seven days a week. God gave us the Sabbath day, a day of rest.

Here's the challenge: rest is not valued in our culture.

We value productivity and achievement more highly. We cheer on those who are busy, those who get things done. Workaholics are admired. Sitting still is for lazy people, right? But we ignore the warning signs of a tired body at our peril. Without rest, we get sick. We need to intentionally and carefully manage our physical capacity and our body's need for regular, quality rest.

There is now so much science that supports the importance of quality sleep for our health. It's right at the top of the list. But when was the last time you had eight hours of uninterrupted sleep? Was it this week? This month?

I'm learning how to manage my physical energy levels. I limit how often I go out in the evening each week. If I'm out too often in the evening, it starts to show. Sometimes I have had to decline invitations and miss out on events because I know my physical limits, and I know what happens when I get too tired. On the weekend, I allow myself the luxury of sitting still without guilt to give my body a rest and recharge for the week ahead.

Hand in hand with physical rest is physical exercise. I know that when my body is fit and strong, it improves every other part of my life—every other. But I still struggle to put in the time and energy I should to exercise. This is in the 'room for improvement' category.

Mental

I find some tasks use a lot of brain power. Writing is one of them, as well as developing Bible study resources, strategic planning, and detailed data entry. I get to the stage where I start making silly mistakes, struggle to think creatively and hit a mental block. I now know not to panic, not to give up with an "I can't do it" feeling of failure, but to take a break and stop thinking for a while.

When I'm stuck on a complex problem, when I can't find the right words, the best thing I can do is stop and do something else. I intersperse mentally challenging tasks with mundane physical ones. On writing days, I also get the laundry done, bake sourdough and rearrange houseplants. When I have mentally challenging tasks, I tackle them in time blocks interspersed with coffee with a friend or routine tasks that don't need much brain power. When I get stuck, I clean something or take out my knitting.

I know this is different for different people. I have writer friends who get into a flow and can write for hours on end. I'm not like that. If I have a writing deadline and I have to put in the hours one day, my brain is fried the next. I need to manage my writing assignments carefully because I simply can't write more than 1,000 intelligible words in a day. If I try to, it is like hitting my head against a wall—a useless frustration.

I have heard it said that when you are physically tired, exercise mentally, and when you get mentally tired, exercise physically. This is a great way of thinking. But, there is more to manage than just our physical and mental health.

Emotional

I know my emotional tank is getting low when I find myself internalising and owning other people's problems and hurt. I find it hard to switch off at the end of the day, I have a disproportionate reaction to bad news I see or hear about, and I get highly sensitive to any sniff of relational conflict. Some days it feels like I'm on the verge of bursting into tears at any moment, and it takes all my energy just to keep myself together. That's when I know that my emotional energy jar is empty.

Some people are emotionally exhausting to be around.

They are not necessarily bad people, they are just hard work for me to relate to. Sometimes they ask searching questions or expect something of me. I love them, but after spending time with them, I leave feeling tired.

Other people fill me up. They are easy to be myself around, they love and encourage me, and they make me laugh. (There's nothing like a good laugh to fill up my emotional tank.) These relationships leave me feeling energised. It's important to have both kinds of friends, those who need something from me, and those who pour into me. I just have to manage my relationships with intention and wisdom.

The 24/7 news cycle is emotionally draining for me. Watching the devastation, looking into the eyes of the victims, and hearing the stories of violence, pain and destruction takes a lot out of me. Every day there is another shooting, another war begins, another cyclone hits, another flood rises, another, and another, and another. Every day. Another.

There was one stage when we regularly had the news channel on in the background at home. Not anymore. The headlines are enough. And even then, it doesn't need to be every day.

The best way for me to keep my emotional tank full is to spend time with my family. I am very blessed to have a wonderful marriage and kids who get along well with each other and their partners. Spending time with them makes me feel proud, loved and content. So, it's important that I spend time with my family.

My marriage is a life-giving relationship for me. I am so blessed to still be married after thirty-two years and to still be having fun with my guy. There have been difficult seasons, for sure. But investing in my marriage relationship has been worth every effort. Murray and I still go on a date regularly. When our children were young, our date nights were less frequent. We hired a babysitter at least once a month to get out of the house and have a quality conversation. When they were in high school and old enough to go to youth group on Friday night, we started dating. We would drop the kids off at church at 6 pm for their program, and rather than go home to watch TV, we went out for dinner. Even now, long after our children have grown up and left home, we still go out on a date most Friday nights. This routine helps us stay connected as husband and wife, it gives us something to look forward to during the week, and it helps top up my emotional energy supply.

A funny movie, a good book, an unhurried conversation with a friend all keep my emotional energy tank filled up.

Spiritual

Spiritual energy is the one that I find most difficult to be aware of until I start to get low. God calls us to a life that is beyond our own capacity so we can be constantly dependent on Him. I get spiritually depleted when I am busy in ministry, doing what God called me to, without being completely plugged into the source of my calling.

Jesus said:

> *I am the vine; you are the branches. If you remain in me and I in you, you will bear much fruit; apart from me you can do nothing. If you do not remain in me, you are like a branch that is thrown away and withers; such branches are picked up, thrown into the fire and burned.*[45]

A withered branch is exactly what I feel like when I neglect to abide in Him.

I know I am spiritually depleted when I find myself being a people pleaser, making decisions to keep people happy so they like me. I see the problems around me but can't quite picture the power of God to overcome them. When people come to me for help or prayer, and my heart responds with a sigh instead of a smile, I know I'm running low. When I constantly feel inadequate for the task, I know I am relying on my own strength rather than the strength of the Holy Spirit in me. Outside of Christ, I don't have the capacity to love, to forgive, to be gentle and kind. These things are the fruit of the Spirit, not the fruit of trying harder.

I need to invest time in my spiritual health. A quick daily Bible reading and a rote prayer don't make much of an impact on my spiritual energy. The spiritual disciplines that keep my spiritual jar filled are just that, disciplines. I refill by spending time in God's Word, meditating on God's character and love.

I have recently discovered the joy of Scripture writing; slowing right down and taking the time to physically form each word on the page of a notebook. Writing out passages of Scripture helps me see patterns and themes I miss when I just read or listen to the words. Writing out longhand the things God is teaching me in His word, His challenge and encouragement to me, focuses my mind on Him, magnifying His power and making my own shortcomings insignificant.

I also need to spend time in prayer, offload the burdens of my heart, and quietly listen to the voice of the Spirit speaking courage and truth into my life. And my perspective shifts. As I meditate on the character of God, my problems become smaller, and I have the faith to believe in miracles once again.

1 Peter 5:7 reminds me:

Cast all your anxiety on him because he cares for you.

When I am intentional about handing my concerns to God, it builds my faith and fills my spiritual energy.

There is a fascinating insight into Jesus' ministry we see in the account of the healing of the woman who had been bleeding for twelve years. Jesus was busy, on His way to heal Jairus' daughter. As the crowds bustled around Him, the woman touched the hem of Jesus' garment and was healed. Jesus knew immediately. "I know that power has gone out from me."[46] Jesus immediately recognised when He was being depleted of healing energy. He was aware. He was filled by spending time alone with His Father, and He expended the energy in healing and ministry.

The gospels remind us that Jesus didn't just keep going and going and going. He regularly took breaks away to rest, to pray, to be still. Jesus knew how to manage His energy levels.

And He taught His disciples to do the same. In the middle of a busy season of ministry, preaching and healing, Jesus received word that His cousin, John the Baptist, had been killed. At this point, Jesus didn't ignore the toll that grief takes; rather, He planned a time of rest.

"Come away with me to a quiet place and rest."[47]

What a beautiful invitation.

***

I read a story in Wayne Cordeiro's book Leading on Empty[48] that continues to have a significant impact on me. Cordeiro tells the story of a farmer who had a roadside stall of farm fresh produce: milk, eggs, tomatoes, and cheese. As the customers lined up to purchase his quality produce, eventually things would run out. He responded to the disappointed customers by calmly saying, "Come back tomorrow and I'll have more."

It didn't matter how great the customers' need for fresh milk was that day, once the day's supply was sold, there was no choice but to wait until the next day when the cow was milked again.

This concept doesn't only apply to physical products. It applies to our internal resources as well. People will continue to line up and request more and more from us, but at some point, we must be able to say, "I don't have any more. Come back tomorrow." When we are empty, we don't have to apologise. We have to refill.

All of this may seem very simple and common sense, and it is. The trouble is that our lives are so busy and demanding that we often don't take the time to take an inventory and think about how we're travelling. We push on and on until we run dry. Empty.

This reality of limited capacity doesn't sit well. I feel like I'm letting people down. I feel like I should be able to do more. I say yes to things when I don't have time to do them well. I keep piling on the pressure to get more done until I'm so overwhelmed and stressed I can't function properly.

But God knew I could only do so much, and the pressure to get more done every day does not come from Him. My desire to keep everyone happy is my own burden, not God's. It comes from my pride, my longing to be accepted and admired. God doesn't expect more from me than what He created me to be able to do. He knew my limits when He called me to be a wife, mother, pastor and friend. He knew I wouldn't be enough, and that is fine because, in all things, He is enough.

We can lay our burden down and rely on our all-sufficient

God to fill the gap between our best efforts and everything He is doing. We are not designed to be able to do it all alone. We are supposed to need Him.

God can multiply what we have when we give it to Him and let it be enough. Jesus was constantly challenging the disciples to lift their expectations beyond what was normal to what God was capable of—more than they could ever imagine. When Jesus asked His disciples to feed a hungry crowd, they came up with all the excuses of why it couldn't be done. They were too far away from the town, they didn't have enough money, there were too many people, it simply wasn't possible. End of story.

But Jesus asked them a simple question, "What do you have?" You've told me all about what you don't have. Now, tell me what you have. What is in your hands?

"Two loaves and five fish" was the answer. Enough food for one or two, useless under the circumstances with thousands of hungry people to feed. It wasn't enough to warrant mentioning. There was no way what they had could ever meet the need. Until they gave it to Jesus. Jesus could take an amount so small it wasn't worth mentioning and turn it into an abundance. Jesus not only satisfied the hunger of the people, but there were leftovers. God provided more than enough. And just so we didn't miss the miracle, He did it again on another day with another crowd and another measly lunch box.

Jesus isn't asking us to be more than we can be or do more than we can do. He's asking us to give the teensy amount we have to Him and trust Him to provide what He has called us to. God is asking us to take our eyes off our inadequacy and focus on His power and provision, His ability to take what isn't worth mentioning and create an abundance, more than we need.

This is so hard to do. I tend to be overwhelmed by the whinging of the hungry crowd and forget that God is even there, let alone has the power to provide what I can't. I feel responsible for meeting the needs around me. It feels like my job to fix things. But there are so many times in life when the resources we have in our hands are grossly insufficient.

As a pastor and friend, I never had enough time or energy to cook enough meals, sit by enough hospital beds or have the right words of comfort and hope to truly make a difference. As a parent, I couldn't fix the heartaches my children had to overcome. As a wife, I couldn't love my husband the way he needs. I could never be good enough. But God, by His love and grace, has filled in the gap. And He is enough.

The miracle may not be as obvious or spectacular as feeding five thousand people with a single lunch, but when I look at my kids now, I know it is only by God's grace they have grown up to be the adults they are. God has filled the gap in my marriage. God has filled the gap in my ministry. And God continues to fill the gaps in my limited capacity every day.

We need to rely on God to make what we have enough, and we also need each other in a community of faith. We are not designed to be self-sufficient. We need each other.

"Let me know if there is anything I can do to help."

We say it to each other all the time. But when was the last time you accepted help? When have you answered, "That would be great! Can you pick up the kids from school on Tuesday?" or, "Can you bring dinner around one night this week?" If you're anything like me, you say thank you and then never ask.

I was chatting to my mum recently. On Friday afternoon, she received a phone call from my sister, Joanne, asking if she was busy on Saturday morning. Apologising for the short notice, Joanne asked Mum to help her prepare her home for her son's eighteenth birthday party that evening. So, Mum spent her Saturday morning folding laundry, dusting and vacuuming with her youngest daughter. They both had fun, and the jobs got done quickly and easily. Could Joanne have managed to do everything by herself? Yes, she could have. But it was better done together.

We are not failing at life when we ask for help. It's not a bad thing to need each other. God meant for us to be part of families and communities, to lift each other up and lighten the load, especially during seasons of need.

We can look at the limits of our capacity as a burden, but what if it is also a gift? What is the upside of not being able to do it all? John Mark Comer talks about how our limitations can be signposts that guide us to discover God's will for our lives.[49] We can't do everything; we have to make choices. We have to find the limited number of things that are truly ours to accomplish.

Our limits force us to live deliberately, prioritising the things that are truly important. There are some things that only we can do, like loving our own family and caring for our own household. So, when we spend too much energy doing unnecessary things outside of our essentials, we end up neglecting the people we love the most. When we jump wholeheartedly after every exciting opportunity that comes across our path, we find ourselves spread so thin the joy disappears from even the activities we love. We have to be able to say no.

God knows we have limited capacity. He never intended us to do everything for everyone, to carry the weight of the world on our shoulders and keep everyone happy. No, He knew what we could bring would be inadequate for our lives. That's the way He designed us to be—totally reliant on Him.

Let's not burn ourselves out trying to do it all. Let's manage our energy carefully, ensuring we have the reserves we need. Let's trust in God's miraculous provision to fill the gap between what we have to give and what He is calling us to. And let's make wise and intentional decisions about how to use the limited time and energy we have, devoting ourselves to the things that are truly most important.

TAKE TIME TO REFLECT

☼ Do you feel like you should be doing more? Are there always more things on your to-do list than time in your day?

☼ Do you feel obliged to volunteer to help every time the request is made? Does your family get the dregs of your energy at the end of the day?

Here are some practical steps to lay this burden down:

- Do an energy inventory. Over the next few weeks, note the activities that drain your energy and the activities that refill your energy.

- Identify the things that are draining and plan some refilling activities before and after.

- Block out recovery time after busy seasons and gift yourself the rest you need.

- Where you feel inadequate, give what you have to God and ask Him to miraculously provide.

10

GOOD GIRL CHRISTIAN

THE BURDEN OF RELIGION

I was ten days old the first time I went to church, and I've barely missed a service since. I grew up in a loving Evangelical family; my father has been a pastor all my life. I gave my heart to Jesus kneeling by my bed with my mother and sister after church one Sunday evening as a very young child. I never rebelled against God or walked away from my faith as a teenager or young adult. I was a very boring Christian, with a very boring testimony.

Up until a few years ago, I spent all my discretionary time in church activities, and I didn't have time for meaningful friendships outside of the church. Everyone I knew was a Christian. My kids were in a Christian school. I worked in a Christian environment. I lived in a Christian bubble.

And it was exhausting.

On the outside, I was doing everything right. I was in church every Sunday, and life group every Wednesday night. I went to prayer meetings and working bees. I prayed and read my Bible and put money in the offering. I was trying as hard as I could to be the very best Christian I could be. But I had a nagging dissatisfaction. I secretly wondered if this was the abundant life Jesus promised me. Because if it was, I was disappointed. Although, I would never admit that to anyone.

When I had my chest pain and was forced to re-evaluate my life, my husband encouraged me to take a step back from ministry. It was too much. It wasn't sustainable or healthy. My counsellor encouraged me to take an extended break. But I knew that taking a break would not change anything in the long term; I would come back to the same pressure, busyness and stress.

I struggled to rationalise: I was doing God's work, following God's call on my life, obediently sacrificing myself for the sake of the Kingdom, and yet, I wasn't happy or healthy. How could this be? It didn't make sense.

Until I dared to step away and discover what my faith looked like outside of the organised church.

When we were on our trip around Australia, we tried going to some local churches. We would look up the service times online and show up ten minutes early, like all visitors. We would sit by ourselves through the service and then sit awkwardly afterwards while people around us greeted their friends. And then we would leave. Sometimes not one person said hello other than the designated greeter at the door. It was depressing. So we stopped going. We watched the live stream of our old church from home unless we were in a town where we could go to church with friends or family we knew.

On Sunday afternoons we would find a local brewery or pub. Australia has some iconic pubs around the country with so much history and character they are must-visit destinations. And often, they were also some of the friendliest places. Locals would strike up a conversation and be genuinely interested in who we were and where we had been. They told us their life stories and invited us to be a part of their community for the short time we were there. We felt welcome and included. I wonder if this is why Jesus spent time with 'tax collectors and sinners.' He ate with them. He welcomed them.

It made me realise that the church world isn't necessarily the real world, and, sadly, church people aren't always very good at living like Jesus.

***

I need to make a distinction here, because although the line is often blurry, there is a difference between religious practice and a personal relationship with Jesus. It does get confusing though, because there are things on both sides of the line and it's hard to distinguish from the outside which side I'm on. Often the only difference is the motivation of my heart.

Take spiritual disciplines, for example. Spiritual disciplines are good; they are important for our spiritual growth and faith journey. It is part of our sanctification process, making us more and more like Jesus. Spiritual disciplines include things like Bible reading, prayer, giving, fasting and sharing our faith. They are all important things to do as Christ's followers.

These practices bring us closer to God. They make our relationship stronger and richer. We learn and grow and exercise our faith through these practices. But the problem is that we turn them into boxes to tick and obligations to fulfil. Before we know it, we are trying to manipulate the favour of God by behaving in a certain way. We flip the motivation from relationship to religion.

Humanity has always had the propensity to religiosity. We find it so often in the Bible. God gave His people clear rules to follow so they could live in relationship with Him. After being in slavery for four hundred years, the Israelites didn't have a strong social structure to guide them, so God gave them one. It was quite an involved system of regulations and sacrifices. You can read the Law in Deuteronomy and Leviticus. The headlines are in the Ten Commandments.

By the time Jesus entered the picture a few hundred years later, the Pharisees and religious leaders had added layers of rules around the original rules God had given them, apparently to protect people from getting close to breaking the rules. The problem was that the new rules turned into a show. Their life became a performance of religious practices and rituals to prove how godly they were, and they forgot the God whom they served.

So when Jesus arrived, He didn't get on very well with the religious leaders of His day. In fact, they clashed constantly. And eventually, those were the guys that put Jesus to death because they found Him so threatening. Jesus came to show us what God was really like, and His life wasn't a performance of religious rituals. What did Jesus do? He loved people the religious leaders cast aside, He fed the hungry and healed the sick. And He broke a lot of rules.

Jesus brought the Law back to its original intent: Love God and love each other.

Love the Lord your God with all your heart, mind and strength, and love your neighbour as yourself.[50]

This is how to follow God. This is the most important thing.

Sounds great! Let's all do that.

Our churches have tried to be helpful by organising programs and events for us to follow. There are multiple church services to attend each week. There are Bible studies and prayer meetings for us to go to. They publish Bible reading plans and devotionals to keep up with, develop evangelism classes to learn how to share the gospel in four tidy spiritual laws and prayer triplets to keep us accountable. I may sound a little sarcastic but I'm not. I've spent my life developing and participating in these religious practices. I love this stuff. This is my comfort zone.

But my faith was different when I wasn't plugged into the program of organised church. And I discovered a vitality and depth I hadn't experienced before. Jesus is not contained within the walls of a church building, and a relationship with Him cannot be programmed.

I have extended family who are an active part of their church. They are also avid classic car enthusiasts. And several guys from their church also love classic cars. The problem is that the local car club meets monthly on a Sunday. The choice is, A: skip the church service once a month and build a relationship with guys in the community around a shared passion, or B: start a new classic car club on Saturdays for the church guys. What would Jesus do? Is this the line where going to church on Sunday becomes a religious practice rather than being the body of Christ?

For almost all my life, I would have started the Saturday car club. No question. There is no other acceptable option.

You can't skip church on purpose. Church attendance is a number one priority for a good Christian.

But that black-and-white, right-and-wrong rule system of living my faith isn't sitting so well in my spirit anymore.

Both of my daughters were born on a Saturday, and I missed out on going to church because I was still in hospital. So when my son was born on a Tuesday, I was determined not to miss a service. Five days after giving birth to my third child, a two and a three-year-old in tow, I was back in church. What was I thinking? Was I thinking of my healing body, my little girls struggling to adjust to the new family dynamic or a longing to worship Jesus? No. I was thinking of the round of applause. I was thinking about what other people were thinking. I wanted to appear to be a good Christian. It was all about religion and not a bit about my relationship with Jesus. I would yell at my family all morning to get them out the door on time so we could smile in our Sunday best and look like the perfect family when we arrived at church.

I still believe going to church regularly and being involved in a local church family is vitally important for our faith. I've heard it said you don't need to go to church to be a Christian, and I disagree. Being a part of a good church where we can worship together with other believers, listen to God's Word being taught, support local and global missions, be involved in serving the local community and be held accountable for the way we live are important aspects of our faith that we can't do alone. The church needs me, and I need the church, within the broader context of life and faith.

***

An expert in the Jewish Law asked Jesus one day, "What must I do to inherit eternal life?" The passage tells us that this man wanted to test Jesus. His question wasn't genuine. He didn't want to know the answer; he wanted to catch Jesus out. So, just like Jesus did many times before, rather than answering, He asked another question. "What is written in the Law?"

The Law expert gave Jesus the right answer. I talked about it earlier:

> *"Love the Lord your God with all your heart and with all your soul and with all your strength and with all your mind"*; and, *"Love your neighbour as yourself."*[51]

Love God. Love each other. That's it.

The expert's follow-up question was, "Who is my neighbour?" Again, Jesus didn't give him a straight answer. He told a story. We know it as the parable of the Good Samaritan. In this story, a man was robbed and left for dead on the notoriously dangerous road between Jerusalem and Jericho. But then others found him, first a priest and then a Levite. Now, the priest and the Levite were the religious elite of the day, like a pastor and a deacon, or an evangelist and a Sunday school teacher. These were the people who were the leaders in their faith community. They were the good guys.

But, of course, the one who took the time and gave the money to care for the injured man was a Samaritan. He was an outcast in their community. The Samaritan man was not welcome at their dinner table or in their worship service.

The expert in the law got the message, although I'm sure he wasn't too happy about the encounter. When Jesus asked him, who was the good neighbour, he rightly answered, "The one who had mercy." And Jesus told him, "Go and do likewise."

This is what Jesus teaches us true religion looks like.

It's not easy for us to grasp the full meaning of this story in our time and culture. For a bit of context, if the priest or the Levite had stopped to help the injured man, they would have made themselves ceremonially unclean and would have had to go through a purification ritual before being welcomed back into their religious community. There was a cost. But Jesus is clearly illustrating here that being kind and generous is more important than being ceremonially clean. On the religious priority list, showing love to those in need, even those outside of our culture and religion, is more important than our religious duty. True religion is outward-looking.

Jesus was always getting in trouble with the religious leaders. There are so many passages where Jesus clashes with the Pharisees that I grew up thinking of them as the bad guys, but I was wrong. The Pharisees were the good guys in that community at that time. They were the men who were educated in God's law and devoted their lives to religious piety. They were the leaders of the religious community. They were admired and respected. But they clashed with Jesus.

The Pharisees were devoted to religion, not to God. They didn't have a personal relationship with God; they didn't understand His heart. Their lives were devoted to following a list of rules, not loving people. And Jesus was the opposite. Jesus put people first. He welcomed the lonely, He spent time with people who were caught up in sin—tax collectors, prostitutes, and outcasts. He didn't go around condemning and judging people. He sat and had a meal with them. He welcomed them and healed them. He was 'a friend of sinners'.[52]

James 1:27 tells us:

> *Religion that God our Father accepts as pure and faultless is this: to look after orphans and widows in their distress and to keep oneself from being polluted by the world.*

God wants us to be proactive in looking after those who are less fortunate and to live differently from those who are living without Christ. The purpose of our faith is to bring hope and light into a hopeless and dark world; to serve those who can give us nothing in return. While the world values wealth, we practise generosity. While the world cries, "What about me?" we put others first.

In each of these examples, following God is about caring for the vulnerable. It is outward-looking, and community-facing. It is action-based, generous and kind. There is no reference to church attendance, Bible studies, prayer meetings or singing worship. All of these spiritual disciplines are important. There are plenty of scriptures about them. But when we get to the bottom line, the highest priority, true religion, is not about keeping up with spiritual disciplines, it is all about loving God and loving others.

In the busyness of church life and ministry, I found I tipped the balance in the wrong direction, placing most of my energy and focus on doing religious things rather than simply loving God wholeheartedly and serving others out of an overflow of that love.

Living a religious life, trying to tick all the boxes, is a heavy burden. It's exhausting. We constantly feel like we are not doing enough or keeping up with the list. We never feel like we are good enough. And we aren't, and that's okay because that isn't the point anyway. But if we follow the message that is often preached by our churches, we can inadvertently fall into this religious point-scoring game.

I am no longer employed by the church, so I am not under the same obligation to attend every church service or every prayer meeting and training event. I'm not required to follow the prescribed Bible reading plan or Bible study program. I have a choice on a sunny Sunday morning to either go to church or go to the beach. I usually go to church, but sometimes I go to the beach. Because I have discovered that I connect with God in a tangible way when I am outside in His creation.

I've never been an outdoorsy person. In school, I spent my lunch hours as a library monitor. I wasn't out on the oval playing sport, getting all hot and sweaty. I was in the air-conditioned library, in the quiet, surrounded by books. So it was a surprise to me, when I started travelling in my fifties, how much I enjoyed hiking, fishing and swimming in natural waterholes. It was foreign to me.

When I spent time outside, far away from the comfort of air-conditioned libraries, I discovered a connection with God the Creator I didn't expect. Having lived in a city for so many years, we put a lot of effort into protecting ourselves from nature. Our homes are climate-controlled; we artificially regulate the temperature so we don't feel too hot or too cold. We have screens to keep the bugs out, fences to keep the animals away and carefully manicured gardens with carefully chosen plants. We control our environment, and we limit our exposure to the wild world—the real world.

John Eldredge helps to explain why spending time outside in creation is so important for the health of our soul. He says:

> *You live nearly all your life in a fake world: artificial lighting instead of the warmth of sunlight or the cool of moonlight or the darkness of night itself. Artificial climate rather than the wild beauty of real weather. All the surfaces you touch are things like plastic, nylon, and faux leather instead of meadow, wood, and stream. Fake fireplaces; wax fruit.*

He goes on the say,

God put your soul in this amazing body and then put you in a world perfectly designed for that experience.[53]

Outside the church, I discovered a wild God, a real God. I felt the heat and the cold of the world in my body. I saw waves forming on the far horizon of the Southern Ocean, rolling toward the shore in even lines. I was dwarfed by mountains higher and wider than I could have imagined from the photographs in the brochures. I swam in cold waterfalls on hot days. I saw sharks, crocodiles, manta rays and dugongs. I saw pods of dolphins too numerous to count and emus wading in the shallows with their chicks. I saw fields of wildflowers that no one planted. I experienced the presence of God in a completely new way. It was powerful and real, and I struggle to find the words to articulate the experience.

Our soul comes alive when it is exposed to the real world, the world God created us to inhabit.

Experiencing God outside of the program of the church has helped me see the burden of religion I had been carrying. I now love to go to my regular church service on Sunday to sing in worship, listen to a message from God's Word, and fellowship with my church family. But I also have this whole other avenue of worship and connection with my Saviour. I read my Bible because I love to read the story of love and redemption and to find wisdom for living my life. I love to pray because it is truly like chatting with my best friend. I love to use my spiritual gifts because they build up God's people and fill my days with purpose. And I am much more comfortable having conversations about my faith with people outside the church. It doesn't feel heavy anymore.

TAKE TIME TO REFLECT

- ☼ Does your religious practice feel life-giving, or does it feel like a list of obligations to fulfil?

- ☼ Is the expression of your faith outward-looking and loving to others? Or is all your time taken up inside a Christian bubble?

Here are some practical steps to lay this burden down:

- Have a go at connecting with God in different ways. Try spending time in nature, reading from a different Bible translation and listening to new (and old) worship music.

- Think about your spiritual disciplines and examine your motivation. Are you connecting with God and growing in your faith or keeping up appearances at church?

- Spend time with people outside the church. Practise the way of Jesus, loving people who are not yet in a relationship with Him.

- And, if you're up for it, play hooky one Sunday and enjoy time with God in the real world He created.

11

EVERYONE IS HURTING

THE BURDEN OF SUFFERING

"Can I stay with you for a while?"

It was our daughter, tears in her eyes, suitcases in her hand.

"He doesn't love me anymore."

We hugged. We cried. And my heart smashed into tiny pieces.

It's not supposed to be this way—happily married one day, heartbroken the next.

This happened a month before my panic attack. Two months later, we were in COVID lockdown. We re-arranged the apartment to make room for us all to work from home and created a little cocoon of safety to ride out the storm while our shattered hearts were most raw. It was a long year, but we all got through.

Healing comes.

It wasn't my divorce. It wasn't my pain. But my daughter's trauma hit me hard. My heart broke to see the hopes and dreams of my baby girl in pieces. My heart broke as I lost the relationship with a son-in-law I deeply loved. He was part of our family, and then he was gone.

I took the wedding photos down.

Soon after, our son's best friend from high school took his own life. I sat across the room as Jesse called his friends, one by one, explaining what had happened. There was disbelief, shock, and uncontrolled emotions. We picked them all up and drove them to the COVID-safe funeral. And I watched my son carry the casket of his best friend down the aisle of the chapel and slide it into the back of a shiny black hearse.

I will never get that image out of my head. Every time I hear the song they played, Guy Sebastian's "Choir", I see it again.

We all have our own story of despair. Our lives flip upside down with one phone call, one conversation. The events of a single hour can turn the trajectory of our lives full circle.

It's cancer.

Mum's gone.

There's been an accident.

I can't find a heartbeat.

You have insufficient funds.

You know the list. You can add to it, I'm sure.

Working as a pastor in a large church exposed me to the hurt and pain of many others. I walked alongside families who had lost children. I prayed by hospital beds and gravesides. I cried with those who mourned the loss of loved ones, the loss of marriages, the loss of businesses, the loss of hopes and dreams and family harmony. And over ten years, it took its toll.

I learned after my panic attack of a phenomenon called 'vicarious trauma'. A kind friend who is also a professional in trauma therapy sent me some helpful podcasts to listen to. They described the effect the trauma of others can have on our minds and body. The empathy we have for others who are suffering can trigger a trauma response in us. And when we are exposed to trauma regularly over a long period, this trauma takes its toll.

You don't need to be a pastor to feel the effects of vicarious trauma. We are all exposed to trauma every day; all we need to do is turn on the news. The pain of the entire world is played out for us in real-time and high definition. The graphic images and heartfelt stories grab our hearts, we carry the trauma in our bodies and minds, and it is too heavy to bear.

The question of why a good God can allow so much suffering in the world is one of the big theological debates. Bad things happen to good people all the time. It is all through the biblical narrative, and it is all around us every day. And while the question is impossible to adequately answer, one thing is clear: we cannot carry the hurt of the world on our shoulders. It's too heavy. We need to learn to give it to God.

John Eldredge tells us:

> *You've got to release the world; you've got to release people, crises, trauma, intrigue, all of it. There has to*

be sometime in your day where you just let it go. All the tragedy of the world, the heartbreak, the latest shooting, earthquake—the soul was never meant to endure this. The soul was never meant to inhabit a world like this. It's way too much. Your soul is finite. You cannot carry the sorrows of the world. Only God can do that.[54]

We have to let it go. We have to put it down. But how? How do you live in a world saturated by pain and not feel the weight?

***

Digging into Scripture and understanding where God is in the midst of so much suffering in our world has been an important part of being able to put down the burden of carrying other's pain heavy on my heart.

Genesis 1:31 tells us that when God finished creating the world and everything in it, He said it was 'very good.' At the end of every day of creation, God stands back and considers the work of the day and declares it 'good.' Everything was perfect. There was no pain or death in God's original design. There was no sickness. There were no weeds in the garden or thorns on the roses. Everything was ordered, productive, and alive. Adam and Eve were in perfect relationship with each other and with God, their Creator. They lived in a perfect world. For a little while, anyway.

We don't know how long it took for the serpent to persuade Eve and Adam to eat the fruit God commanded them not to touch. We don't know if it was days or weeks or months. But when they did, the perfection of their world was broken and everything changed. Life got harder. Pain and heartbreak entered the scene. And their relationship with God was also broken. Their sin caused a chasm between them and a holy

God. They could no longer walk with God in the cool of the evening.

Suffering is part of the consequence of sin. Our whole world is broken because of sin.

Often when we think of sin or hear a message in church about sin, we focus on our bad behaviour. We list sins such as greed and gossip, stealing, lying and murder. And, yes, these behaviours are sinful. These are the sins we have to fight the temptation to fall into ourselves. These are the sins we have some control over. But these ungodly behaviours are not the only consequence of sin. Our whole world is tarnished by it.

The world is subject to natural disasters. There are fires, floods, tornadoes and cyclones. There are volcanoes, tidal waves and drought. These global events are out of our control. They are caused by the brokenness of our world, the accumulation of millennia of brokenness.

Another effect of sin is illness. Some risk factors of sickness are within our control. The way we take care of our bodies affects our health. But healthy people who take care of themselves also get sick. My brother-in-law, a healthy fifty-two-year-old man, was found to have lung cancer. They found the tumour with a chest X-ray he needed for a routine medical exam when he applied for a new job. There were no symptoms. There were no lifestyle risk factors. He didn't smoke. He wasn't overweight. There is no reasonable explanation. It just happens. It happens because our world is broken. It is not the way God designed it to be. God didn't create it this way or plan for us to live in pain. It is a repercussion of our rebellion against God.

Before we move on, let me make an important distinction: pain is a consequence of sin—it is not the punishment for sin. God doesn't punish us for our sins by sending sickness or natural disasters our way. We don't get struck by lightning for bad behaviour.

Many sins have natural consequences. I remember telling my two-year-old daughter not to touch the stove because it was hot. Do you think she believed anything I told her? No, she had to prove it for herself. So she suffered the natural fallout of her disobedience—a burnt hand. When we disobey God's wisdom in our lives, we suffer the natural consequences of our choices.

But when bad things happen to people, it isn't because God is punishing them for some secret sin in their lives. Sin has permeated every part of our world, and no one avoids its effects.

Jesus took the penalty for our sins. He paid the price, in full. Our sins are not held against us. God says He has removed our sins "as far as the East is from the West."[55] That's a long way. We don't carry our guilt. We are free in Christ. God is not making us suffer as a punishment for our disobedience.

When we are in the middle of our suffering or bombarded by the suffering of those around us, it can be difficult to have an eternal perspective. Pain has a way of keeping us blind to everything outside of the present moment. But it is important to remember that our suffering is not forever—it will come to an end.

Our lives are short in comparison to eternity. And when our lives on earth are over, so is our suffering. We can look forward to an eternity where everything is put right, the way God intended it to be. No matter what we face here on earth, it will pass.

Jesus promises us that there will be a day when there is no more suffering or pain, no more tears or death or darkness. Oh, what a wonderful day that will be!

Paul has an amazing mindset. Although he suffered, he was able to keep an eternal perspective, declaring that his suffering in this world does not compare to the glory of eternity.

> *I consider that our present sufferings are not worth comparing with the glory that will be revealed in us.*⁵⁶

The Apostle Paul knew his suffering wasn't wasted. He had no regrets about the cost he paid for his faith and the opposition and hardship he endured because of it. Paul kept his eyes on Heaven and gained encouragement from knowing that what he was going through wasn't the end of the story. The end of the story he was living through had been written. We know how the battle we are fighting ends. That reality doesn't diminish our pain, but it does change our perspective while we persevere.

***

While I don't think God causes bad things to happen per se, He does use the things that happen in our lives for good. There are several references to this in Scripture.

Joseph was a young man who was spoiled as a child because his father, Jacob, loved his mother, Rachel, better than his other three wives. Who would have guessed that polygamy would cause difficult family dynamics? Joseph's ten brothers, born from Jacob's other wives, hated Joseph so much that they faked his death and sold him to slave traders.

Joseph had a roller coaster of a life. He went from favourite son, to slave, to the head of Potiphar's household, to being falsely accused of rape and sent to prison, to then becoming the Prime Minister of all of Egypt.

Eventually, when Joseph came face-to-face with the brothers who had sold him into slavery he said, "You intended to harm me, but God intended it for good to accomplish what is now being done, the saving of many lives."⁵⁷ In hindsight, Joseph recognised the hand of God in bringing him into the position of power and influence that ultimately saved the lives of his family.

And I can say the same thing about my life. My life does not resemble that of Joseph at all, but I can definitely look back and see how God has used difficult seasons to propel me forward into places that were better than I could have ever imagined or planned on my own.

We left our former church after fourteen years. It was the church where our kids grew up, I was on staff in a ministry team I loved, and my husband was part of the senior leadership team. And then there were circumstances beyond our control that meant we needed to leave. It was agonising.

We moved to a much larger church, a place with a thriving youth group for our kids to build great friendships into their teenage years, and a place where Murray and I could hide, and heal. I remember thinking as I walked in, "They don't need me here." Of course, I was wrong. A year later I was invited to join the pastoral team where I served for over ten years. They did need me. I grew so much in those years. And I discovered a purpose far beyond what I would have put my hand up for without the pushing along of the Holy Spirit through the difficulties that led us there.

Did God cause the split in our previous church? No way. I'm sure that season broke God's heart just as much as it broke ours. But did God use it to bring our family to somewhere even better? Yes, by His grace, He did. God used something terrible to bring about something good.

I was collaborating with an old colleague on a project recently. We were writing Bible study materials for our church series on miracles and reflecting on times when God didn't answer our prayers for miracles, and yet, God did miracles in other ways that were just as amazing. She was sharing about the time when her father died of cancer five years prior. God did not answer the prayer for healing. Her father died, just as the doctors predicted he would. But God did miracles in their family, nonetheless. Broken relationships were healed, love flourished, and those who were far away from God were restored to faith. God was at work during a painful time for their family, and He brought about something good.

***

God does not cause our suffering, God does good things through our suffering, and God is with us in our suffering. I find this truth profoundly comforting. No matter where we are, day or night, at our best or at our worst, God is with us. This is the very nature of God. And there are so many scriptures that remind us of this truth.

One of my favourite verses is Joshua 1:9. I shared about it before. It is part of the handover of leadership from Moses to Joshua. Moses had been a great leader and a friend of God. He had spoken to God face-to-face, to the extent that Moses' face shone because of the time he spent in God's presence. Joshua had been Moses' right-hand man for many years and had seen God at work, from the escape from Egypt all the way to the Promised Land. But being the 2IC is different to being the man in charge. So God gave Joshua special encouragement:

> *Have I not commanded you? Be strong and courageous. Do not be afraid; do not be discouraged, for the Lord your God will be with you wherever you go.*[58]

Did you catch the bottom line? God said, I will be with you. Through all the ups and downs of leadership, I'm going to be here, by your side.

David the Psalmist wrote in one of the most famous chapters of the whole Bible, Psalm 23:

Surely your goodness and love will follow me all the days of my life.[59]

David was a shepherd. He had a flock of sheep following him wherever he went. He knew about following. We had a dog that would follow me wherever I went. That was, unless my daughter, Amy, was home, and then the dog would follow Amy. Stella would curl up under the desk, leaning against my feet. And if I moved to the kitchen, or the laundry, or outside, Stella would follow. She spent her whole life following whomever she loved most around our home.

This is what God is like. His goodness and love follow us wherever we go. Hot on our heels when we walk; leaning against us when we sit down, offering comfort, protection, wisdom and care.

When the angel appeared to Mary to announce the coming of the Messiah, he declared that "'His name will be called Emmanuel' (which means, 'God with us')."[60] That's right. The name given to our Saviour means God is with us. Jesus is the person of God. He lived among us and showed us what God is like.

And the promise continues.

When Jesus returned to Heaven, He gave the promise "I am with you always, to the very end of the age."[61] We are not abandoned. We are not alone. Fifty days later, God sent the gift of His Spirit and called Him "The Comforter." Yes, the presence of God's Spirit with us is comfort.

God is with us, wherever we go, whatever we do. We cannot escape the presence of God. We are never alone. We don't have to face any pain by ourselves.

At the end of Romans chapter eight, Paul gives us this wonderful encouragement:

> *For I am convinced that neither death nor life, neither angels nor demons, neither the present nor the future, nor any powers, neither height nor depth, nor anything else in all creation, will be able to separate us from the love of God that is in Christ Jesus our Lord.*[62]

Nothing can get between us and God. He is with us, He follows us, He dwells with us. In our suffering, God is present.

* * *

We often can't choose if, when or how we suffer, but at some time or another everyone goes through hard times. Some people become bitter in their pain. For some people, their suffering becomes part of their identity. For others, however, their hardship gives them empathy and they become more Christlike. The truth is, we can choose how we respond to suffering.

You probably know people whose suffering has made them bitter and others who have become better. We can, with God's help, take the hardships we face and grow stronger in our faith, developing a stronger relationship with our God through it all.

The Apostle Paul was well acquainted with suffering. He suffered terrible injustice and hardship during his life in ministry. Yet, he knew that the fruit of his hardship was valuable.

> *We also glory in our sufferings, because we know that suffering produces perseverance; perseverance, character; and character, hope.*[63]

James, the brother of Jesus expressed the value of suffering like this:

Consider it pure joy, my brothers and sisters, whenever you face trials of many kinds, because you know that the testing of your faith produces perseverance. Let perseverance finish its work so that you may be mature and complete, not lacking anything.[64]

These men of God knew that their character and faith could be strengthened by the lessons they learned during the difficult seasons of life. There is not one Olympic competitor or elite sportsman or woman who has gotten to the top of their field without pain. Pain is part of the strengthening process.

And then, we can use what we learn to help others. When we learn and grow through the difficult experiences in our lives we can empathise and encourage others who are still neck-deep in their pain. There is so much value in knowing we are not alone when difficulty strikes. God comforts us so that we can comfort others with the comfort we have received from God.[65]

A community of others who care and support us through whatever we are facing makes an enormous difference. We have a group of widows at our church who have formed a little club. They call themselves 'The Rubies' after Proverbs 31:10. Pastors, friends and families can offer all the kind words and casseroles in the world, but there is nothing as helpful as a conversation with others who have walked the same road.

Drug addiction clinics are staffed with recovered addicts. Divorce support groups are led by divorcees. The best breast care nurses have recovered from breast cancer themselves. All the training in the world can't substitute having been through the experience. And no one gets the experience without walking through the pain, one step at a time.

***

Writing about suffering is hard. This has not been a fun chapter. Thanks for sticking with me. It's not easy, but I think we need to talk about suffering more often. By not talking openly about suffering, we can be left with the impression that people who suffer have either brought it on themselves somehow or that God has abandoned them, when quite the opposite is true. God is close to us in our heartache. It is not a burden we have to carry heavily, or alone.

In fact, we can create space for it in our lives rather than ignoring its possibilities and being blindsided when it comes along. Suffering is inevitable, but we rarely give ourselves room to deal with it. We are already overburdened and maxed out. When we are already living in survival mode, any crisis that comes along brings the whole apple cart down, like the news of my daughter's divorce. I was already stressed out to the limit, and I didn't have the space to process what was happening in a healthy way.

When we learn to lay down the other burdens and are living freely and lightly, when we have breathing room in our calendar and healthy levels of emotional energy, we have so much more capacity to cope with the unexpected curve balls that life sends our way.

Helen Keller wrote:

> *Although the world is full of suffering, it is full also of the overcoming of it.*[66]

We cannot avoid the difficulties of life, but we can focus on overcoming them.

TAKE TIME TO REFLECT

☼ Are you weighed down by suffering? Do you struggle to manage the effects of trauma?

☼ Do you deeply feel the hurt of others when you see them in pain? Do you struggle to function normally when you hear bad news?

Here are some practical steps to lay this burden down:

- Meditate on the promises of God. Focus on the comfort of God and use these promises to guide your prayers.

- Look for hidden miracles. It may not be evident at the time, but God is at work in and through every difficult circumstance.

- Reach out for support. Do not suffer alone. Seek out a friendship group or professional support agency to help you process and heal.

12

A NEW BEGINNING

LEARNING TO LIVE FREELY AND LIGHTLY

"Where do you want to go next?"

We planned our trip around the country in three-month blocks with short visits home to see family and friends in between. This pattern worked well, giving us enough of a plan to feel settled and enough flexibility to go and see places we didn't know existed until we were on the doorstep.

I wasn't surprised by the question. But I was reluctant to share the honest answer. We had been on the road for two and a half years and had explored more of our country than I ever imagined possible. Most people who tackle 'the lap' do it in six to nine months. But we had done it slowly, taking in the personality of each new town we visited and making friends along the way.

"I think I want to go home."

I loved our life on the road. I loved discovering new places. I loved slow conversations with strangers, spending my days outdoors in beautiful places and my evenings reading or knitting in our cozy little van. Life was simple and had a nice balance of adventure and predictability. And I didn't know what we would be going home to.

I shouldn't have been surprised by Murray's reaction. He was thinking the same thing as me. We were both ready to return to a more normal life, living in one place, surrounded by family and friends once again.

I remembered what life was like before we left. It was stressful and busy. Days were full of commitments and obligations, weekends were full of errands. I was always busy, always in a hurry, always had too much on my plate. I was stressed out, struggling through each day in survival mode. I knew I didn't want to go back to a life like that. I wanted to be home but live differently from before.

I had learned so much about myself over the last few years. I'm brave and creative, I can learn new things and make big changes. I don't have to mindlessly go with the flow and do the things everyone else is doing. I'd gotten used to living with very few possessions and living at a slower pace.

And I'd learned so much about God. I know what faith looks like outside of the structure of the traditional church. I'd disconnected from the 'profession' of Christianity and discovered a friendship with my Saviour that cannot be programmed or taught in a discipleship class.

So, we began to plan for our return to the city, knowing we wanted to be there, but having no idea what we were going to do or where we were going to live.

What an amazing opportunity! To reinvent our lives. How many people get to do that? The last year has been fascinating as Murray and I have had the freedom to ask ourselves big questions about how we want to live in the next season of our lives. Our nest is empty; we are financially secure. We have a lot of freedom.

What are we going to do with it?

***

While we knew we wanted to be back in Brisbane, close to people we loved, we didn't know where. When we finally set our caravan up in our hometown, we began looking at houses and apartments all over the place. We looked at acreage an hour out of town, we looked at townhouse complexes by the water on the bayside of the city, and we looked at units close to where we used to live in the CBD. We even looked at an over-fifty's retirement community. We honestly had no idea where we wanted to live.

But while the house hunting was going on, Murray had interest from companies wanting him to work for them, and most of the tech companies have offices in the city. We found a suburb close to the centre of town with abundant apartment buildings and good shops, restaurants, cafes and medical facilities, all within walking distance. We narrowed our search to that area.

The first time I walked into our apartment, there were things I liked about it, but I didn't want to live there. It felt too small. It couldn't accommodate our family dining table. The kitchen had little storage and even less bench space.

There was no separate study space for me to write or sew. It was tiny. And after spending almost three years in a twenty-one-foot caravan, I was ready to spread out a little and have my own space.

This apartment has now been our home for a year and a half, and we love it.

The first thing we did was to paint the walls a creamy eggshell colour and replace the worn bedroom carpet. We sold our big family dining table and replaced it with a much smaller one. We bought a bed with storage underneath it where our out-of-season clothes and Christmas decorations now live. I found an inspiration photo on Pinterest and carefully created a living room we would love to come home to.

While we were travelling, we kept our most precious possessions in a shed at the back of a family member's home. We didn't know how long we would be gone for, so I stored my good work clothes and shoes, books and photo albums, my quilt fabric stash and good kitchenware. Fifteen boxes that held what we treasured most about our old lives.

But while we were away, there was a flood in our hometown, and the shed where our boxes were stored was inundated. We were on the other side of the country at the time and couldn't do anything about what happened. Our family back home did an amazing job of keeping what they could, washing it and repacking it in new boxes. It was a big job, and I am so grateful to them for saving so much.

Yet, opening those boxes triggered emotions I wasn't expecting.

I felt the devastation of the flood all over again, even though it had happened almost two years earlier. I thought I had come to terms with what we had lost. I wasn't prepared for what I found inside each box.

Although everything had been washed and dried out before being repacked, there was a distinct smell and a fine silty mud that covered it all. Everything had to be washed again. Anything that was porous, such as baskets and timber, was covered in mould and had to be thrown away. Few of the shoes and handbags were salvageable.

I just wasn't emotionally prepared. Seeing things we held dear—photos of grandparents now passed away, baskets I had bought at the markets of faraway countries long ago—now in the rubbish pile. As we went through each box, I developed a new appreciation for the family members who dealt with it all when the initial flood happened. They worked so hard to try to save as many of our possessions as possible during a really difficult time for them and their community, and I was overwhelmed with gratitude.

I developed a new empathy for others who lost so much more than we did. I had never really been impacted by a natural disaster before. We lost little compared to others who had the flood go through their homes. They lost everything in one fell swoop. I can't even imagine what that would be like.

Despite that, I wasn't prepared to relive the flood, and I wasn't emotionally prepared to confront my past life. I remember opening a box of coat hangers. There must have been 100 timber hangers in this one big mover's box. That's how many clothes we used to have hanging in our closet, and at the time it felt very normal. I looked at the pile and burst into tears. I know my response was partly because of the tiredness and stress of moving and unpacking, washing and sorting. But seeing the excess of my past clashed with the new values I had now embraced, and the contrast hit me like a ton of bricks that day. I knew I wanted to live differently. As much as we lost, there was so much more that we still had.

It could have been a lot worse. And, having lived perfectly happily for the past three years without the things in those boxes, we knew that there was nothing we couldn't happily live without.

It's been a year and a half since we purchased that tiny apartment and opened those smelly boxes. It has been a season of living as a minimalist in a materialistic world. It has been a season of living slowly and simply when everyone around us is in a hurry, stressed and busy. It has been a season of reconnecting with our family, finding our place in a new church and making new friends. It's been a season of new beginnings.

Is it possible to live an unburdened life? This was my big question coming back to Brisbane. Is Jesus' promise that His yoke is easy and His burden is light achievable? Is it real?

A year and a half down the track I can answer with a resounding, "Yes!" Jesus was for real when He promised us rest for our souls. We can find abundant life, life to the full, when we lay our burdens down.

Here is a little about how I'm learning to lay my burdens down in my new day-to-day life.

***

Within a week of moving into our apartment, I received a call from a pastor asking me to consider applying for a pastoral position on his team. It was perfect for me, in my area of expertise, working for a pastor I admire. It was in a church close to our new home. The old Christine would have taken this invitation as a message from God and jumped right in. But the new Christine took some time to think about how I wanted to be spending my time in this season.

I love pastoral ministry, and I love the church, but I

declined this invitation. This new season requires something different from me. I'm spending the bulk of my time writing. I knew God had called me to write this book and share this message, and I knew it would be difficult to do in the cracks of leftover time if I was working again.

I have maintained a philosophy of slow living. I no longer live in a hurry. I have quiet mornings to sit with my coffee and my Bible. I have time to bake sourdough bread and cook meals from fresh ingredients. I have the time to keep our apartment clean and tidy without having to rush late at night or on weekends. I have margin in my calendar. I live more slowly.

And I have time for my family. I have never been as available for my family as I am now. When my daughter has a day off work and wants to have lunch, I'm there. When my son asks to come over for a homemade meal, it's no problem. We see each of our children regularly and we are involved in their lives again.

We don't have room to have everyone around our kitchen table at the same time, but we've worked out ways to gather. We have a few local restaurants we love to frequent. We can get together, laugh and chat, and we don't have to do the dishes. I would probably prefer to have everyone at home, but that's a compromise I'm happy to make for the other benefits of living where we do.

Our apartment is the smallest place we have ever lived, by far (not including the caravan). But we have everything we need. And we have learned the benefits of living with less. It is not a trade-off that lowers our standard of living. Quite the opposite.

I don't have a stash of extra linen or a spare dinner set for special occasions. I don't have an air fryer or a slow cooker. I don't have a lot of shoes.

But I do have everything I need, and then some.

I still have a stash of yarn for crocheting toys and knitting socks. I still have at least four books on my bookshelf waiting to be read. I have a gallery wall of photographs of our family and our travels. There are throws on my couch and cushions on my bed. And I have a lot of plants—living, growing plants that need to be watered, fertilised and rotated every week or two. I call myself a minimalist, but my home feels cozy and comfortable, and we love living here.

My calendar and my home weren't the only things I needed to reinvent. I also had to buy new clothes when we returned to city life. The shorts or jeans and souvenir T-shirts I had worn during our travels didn't suit my new life, and the work clothes I had kept from when I was a pastor didn't suit this new season either.

New clothes are always fun, but it has also been a challenge. Who is the new me? What does she look like? What does she wear? How much time, effort and money does she spend on her appearance? It has been an interesting exercise.

I buy clothes to fit my body, rather than trying to make my body fit into clothes. My fifty-something-year-old body is wider around the middle than my younger self. And that's okay. Whether I lose weight in future or not, I need clothes to wear that are comfortable and flattering on me right now.

I have good quality, mix-and-match, neutral clothes in my wardrobe. If I'm thoughtful about my consumption, I will be able to go from season to season with minimal updates. I have a simple skincare and makeup routine that uses versatile products. I have found a hairstyle that doesn't take too much maintenance day to day, and I'm not bothered by the silver streaks beginning to come through.

And, now that I feel more comfortable in my own skin, I don't feel as self-conscious anymore. I rarely think about what other people think of me. I don't spend time or energy obsessing over my body. This is much easier to do when I am getting plenty of sleep and eating well. When I feel good, I don't spend as much time thinking about what I look like.

I also don't struggle with worry the way I used to. For many years, the subjects of my worries were my church and my family. And after stepping physically away from both for a season, I have learned that God can take care of them without my help.

Over the past couple of years, I've developed the habit of journalling. First thing every morning, I make myself a cup of coffee and sit quietly with my Bible and my journal. I read a chapter or two of Scripture and write a page in my journal.

There isn't a structure or plan. I begin the page, "Morning, Lord," and then just write whatever comes into my head. Sometimes it is an insightful reflection on Scripture, but often it is a simple account of what is happening in my life and how I'm feeling about it. The practice of slowing down and putting my thoughts and feelings into sentences has a way of untangling my emotions and settling my thoughts. And, in addressing it to God, it becomes a prayer of faith, like my own personal Psalm written each morning. I pour out my heart and then hand it over to God.

I know this is a blessing in this empty nest season of life. I wake up to a quiet home. My husband has his own morning routine, and we have learned to spend this time alone, even though we are both sitting in the same room. I wasn't able to do it when my children were small. I wasn't ever disciplined enough to wake up before the family to spend quiet time with God. It got squashed into the cracks of time I could gather during the day, or the few minutes I sat in the car waiting for the school bell to ring.

I wish I could go back and tell my younger self to stop

feeling guilty about not having enough quiet time with God. I remember always feeling like a bad Christian because my quiet time wasn't quiet. And, rather than just doing what I could when I could, I tried to do it perfectly and felt like a failure when life (in the shape of three tiny humans) inevitably got in the way.

I've found God to be infinitely kinder than I imagined Him to be. He didn't expect my routine to be perfect. He gave me those three tiny humans to care for! Trying to be a better Christian didn't help me become better nearly as much as resting in the presence of my Creator and Saviour, knowing He loved me and wanted the best for me and my family.

Understanding this has helped me grow in self-confidence and resilience. I have realised I will never be enough for some people, and I will always be enough for others. And it has little to do with me. I am who God made me to be. I do what I can. And that is enough.

One thing is for sure: trying to make people happy doesn't bring out the best in me or make me a better person. Rather, concentrating on looking after myself and being the best me that I can be makes me happier, healthier, and more able to contribute to others around me. I am a better person when I stop thinking about what other people think of me.

Jesus does not expect me to solve every problem I hear about or volunteer for every position that becomes available. I have limited energy, and that is the way God designed me to be.

I now have spare capacity in my schedule. I have spare time, ready to be interrupted by opportunities God brings across my path. I can meet young pastors for coffee and encourage them in their ministry. I can join a friend for a difficult doctor's visit or a walk through the farmer's market. I get to do things with my children. And if I get sick, or I'm asked to speak at a ladies' event, I don't need to reshuffle a million things to get myself through. I have margin.

I don't feel like I'm always in the middle of a test, teetering on the brink of failure anymore. I am free. Free to be the me that God created me to be. And He and I work out my schedule together.

My faith no longer consists of a series of tasks to complete and boxes to tick. I attend church regularly with my husband. We have friends there that we share life with. I participate in church life, doing my part to contribute without the pressure and time commitment of vocational ministry.

We also regularly head out of town, spending Sundays with sand under our feet and a fishing rod in our hands, because I know that that is worship too. Spending time in creation, exposed to sun, wind and water, surrounded by living things sustained by the hand of the Creator puts life in perspective.

Politics and economics disappear. There is no one to impress, no to-do list to complete, no reason to check the time. I can be fully present: with myself, with the family and friends we share this time with, and with my Creator.

***

Jesus said to His disciples:

> *Whoever wants to be my disciple must deny themselves and take up their cross and follow me. For whoever wants to save their life will lose it, but whoever loses their life for me will find it.*[67]

For many years I thought this verse meant that to be Jesus' disciple I had to give up everything good and fun and exciting in life and take on all the hardship I could. The harder life was, the better disciple I was. Life was meant to be hard, but Jesus would reward me for my faithfulness through a difficult life and the score would be settled in Heaven.

My understanding of these verses has changed. I now believe a surrendered life is the very best quality of life I will ever experience. Denying myself means denying the desires that will ultimately destroy me, and living for Christ means embracing the best that life can offer.

I am denying myself the need to be in control. I hand over my worries and fears, hopes and dreams. I deny myself the desire to be admired, my longing for material wealth and success. I deny myself the desire to be important, to be the problem solver and saviour of those in need.

I lay it all down. It's heavy and carrying it all is exhausting.

I lay it down and pick up my cross. Because a life with just what Jesus desires for me is a good life. It may not be easy. It will not be void of problems. But I know my God is with me wherever I go, and I know He will supply everything I need. His yoke is easy. His burden is light.

I now know that when I am feeling weary and burdened, when the weight of my life is too heavy, I'm holding onto something that Jesus never intended me to carry.

And so I lay my burdens down.

NOTES

Introduction
1   Matthew 11:28

Chapter One
2   NCLS Research, How Stressed are Australians in 2022?, viewed 17 April 2025, www.ncls.org.au/articles/how-stressed-are-australians/

3   NCLS Research, Baptist Women in Ministry Leadership, viewed 17 April 2025, www.ncls.org.au/media/3voorkk3/ncls_summaryreport_baptist-women-ministry-leadership.pdf

4   R Pendell, Harvard Business Review, Stressed, Sad, and Anxious: A Snapshot of the Global Workforce, viewed 17 April 2025, https://hbr.org/2022/06/stressed-sad-and-anxious-a-snapshot-of-the-global-workforce

5   Gallup, State of the Global Workplace: 2024 Report, viewed 17 April 2025, www.gallup.com/workplace/349484/state-of-the-global-workplace.aspx

6   Quote from the City Cave website explaining float therapy: www.citycave.com.au/float-therapy-main

Chapter Two
7   Mark 10:51

8   Cordeiro, Wayne. 2009. Leading on Empty: Refilling Your Tank and Renewing Your Passion. Minneapolis: Bethany House.

9   Psalm 40:1–2

Chapter Three
10   Quote by Gunner Gundersen posted on Facebook by Tim Challies

11 Comer, John Mark. 2019. The Ruthless Elimination of Hurry: How To Stay Emotionally Healthy and Spiritually Alive in the Chaos of the Modern World. Hodder & Stoughton.

12 Comer, John Mark. 2019. The Ruthless Elimination of Hurry: How To Stay Emotionally Healthy and Spiritually Alive in the Chaos of the Modern World. Hodder & Stoughton.

13 Mark 1:35

14 John 1:43

15 Genesis 2:2–3

16 Exodus 20:8–11

17 Mark 2:27

18 Wanda E. Brunstetter

19 Matthew Kelly

Chapter Four

20 Proverbs 31:30

21 Micah 6:8

22 Ephesians 2:10

23 Luke 10:27

Chapter Five

24 Lucado, Max. 2017. Anxious for Nothing: Finding Calm in a Chaotic World. Nashville: Thomas Nelson.

25 2 Corinthians 10:5

26 Proverbs 3:5–6

27 Luke 10:41-42

28 Matthew 8:23-27

29 Philippians 4:7

Chapter Six

30 Caroline Caldwell

31 Psalm 139:13–14

32 Romans 12:1

33 Romans 12:3

34 Ephesians 2:10

35 Proverbs 31:30

Chapter Seven

36 The Blessing. Kari Jobe, Cody Carnes, Elevation Worship. Graves into Gardens. 2020.

37 Hebrews 4:16

38 1 John 3:1

39 Matthew 7:11

Chapter Eight

40 Mark 10:21

41 Matthew 13:22

42 M MacVean, For many people, gathering possessions is just the stuff of life, Los Angeles Times, 21 March 2014, www.latimes.com/health/la-he-keeping-stuff-20140322-story.html

43 Philippians 4:13

44 Philippians 4:12–13

Chapter Nine

45 John 15:5-6

46 Luke 8:46

47 Mark 6:31

48 Cordeiro, Wayne. 2009. Leading on Empty: Refilling Your Tank and Renewing Your Passion. Minneapolis: Bethany House.

49 Comer, John Mark. 2019. The Ruthless Elimination of Hurry: How To Stay Emotionally Healthy and Spiritually Alive in the Chaos of the Modern World. Hodder & Stoughton.

Chapter Ten

50 Mark 12:30-31

51 Luke 10:27

52 Matthew 11:19

53 Eldredge, John. 2020. Get Your Life Back: Everyday Practices for a World Gone Mad. Nashville: Thomas Nelson.

Chapter Eleven

54 Eldredge, John. 2020. Get Your Life Back: Everyday Practices for a World Gone Mad. Nashville: Thomas Nelson.

55 Psalm 103:12

56 Romans 8:18

57 Genesis 50:20

58 Joshua 1:9

59 Psalm 23:6

60 Matthew 1:23

61 Matthew 28:20

62 Romans 8:38-39

63 Romans 5:3-4

64 James 1:2-4

65 2 Corinthians 1:3-4

66 Keller, Helen. 1903. Optimism. Boston: The Merrymount Press.

Chapter Twelve

67 Matthew 16:24-25

ABOUT THE AUTHOR

CHRISTINE WOOD grew up a pastor's kid in a small town in Central Queensland. She moved to Brisbane to go to university, where she met Murray, her husband of 33 years (and counting).

While their three children were in high school, Christine attended Bible college and trained for vocational ministry, becoming a registered pastor with Queensland Baptists, and serving on the pastoral team at Gateway Baptist Church for over a decade.

Christine knows what it feels like to juggle the relentless demands of marriage, family and ministry, and buckle under the pressure of it all. She has experienced pain and loss and has come out the other side to a life of peace and joy she didn't know was possible.

To read more from Christine, visit
livingwithmargins.com

www.ingramcontent.com/pod-product-compliance
Lightning Source LLC
Chambersburg PA
CBHW020529080526
44583CB00013B/799